Educating and Supporting Autistic Girls is accompanied by a number of printable online materials, designed to ensure this resource best supports your professional needs.

Go to resourcecentre.routledge.com/speechmark and click on the cover of this book.

Answer the question prompt using your copy of the book to gain access to the online content.

Educating and Supporting Autistic Girls

Autistic girls, especially those educated in mainstream environments, have often been missed or misdiagnosed. There is now, however, greater awareness of how autism can present in females, why these girls can remain 'invisible', and what education and health professionals can do to provide better support.

Fully revised and updated, this practical book shines a light on the insights, opinions and experiences of autistic girls and women, providing a rich insight into school life from an autistic perspective. It explores the difficulties and disadvantages that autistic girls can face in educational settings and offers guidance on how to best support them, with a wealth of strategies reflecting good practice in the field of autism and education. The resource also contains a broad range of worksheets and activities on key issues and includes new sections on anxiety, masking, home life, social media, gender and sexual identity.

Key features include:

- A wealth of case studies to illustrate different topics
- Guidance on best practice when working with autistic girls
- New audits to help staff and pupils to identify strengths and areas to improve
- Easy-to-implement strategies and tips to help professionals adapt to environments and policies for autistic students
- Activities and resources for young autistic females to support them in developing self-awareness, coping strategies and learning skills

With the voices of autistic girls and young women woven throughout, drawing upon their experiences of education – from learning and communication, to friendships, transitions and interpreting the world – this is an essential resource for education and health professionals working with autistic girls, particularly in mainstream environments.

Victoria Honeybourne is a neurodiversity specialist, trainer and author with a background in education. She has worked in a number of roles including as a mainstream teacher, senior advisory teacher and autism outreach teacher. Following her own diagnosis, she is particularly passionate about supporting autistic females.

EDUCATING AND SUPPORTING AUTISTIC GIRLS

A Resource for Mainstream Education and Health Professionals

VICTORIA HONEYBOURNE

Designed cover image: © Getty Images

Second edition published 2024
by Routledge
4 Park Square, Milton Park, Abingdon, Oxon, OX14 4RN

and by Routledge
605 Third Avenue, New York, NY 10158

Routledge is an imprint of the Taylor & Francis Group, an informa business

© 2024 Victoria Honeybourne

The right of Victoria Honeybourne to be identified as author of this work has been asserted in accordance with sections 77 and 78 of the Copyright, Designs and Patents Act 1988.

All rights reserved. The purchase of this copyright material confers the right on the purchasing institution to photocopy or download pages which bear the support material icon and a copyright line at the bottom of the page. No other parts of this book may be reprinted or reproduced or utilised in any form or by any electronic, mechanical, or other means, now known or hereafter invented, including photocopying and recording, or in any information storage or retrieval system, without permission in writing from the publishers.

All rights reserved. No part of this book may be reprinted or reproduced or utilised in any form or by any electronic, mechanical, or other means, now known or hereafter invented, including photocopying and recording, or in any information storage or retrieval system, without permission in writing from the publishers.

Trademark notice: Product or corporate names may be trademarks or registered trademarks, and are used only for identification and explanation without intent to infringe.

First edition published by Routledge 2016

British Library Cataloguing-in-Publication Data
A catalogue record for this book is available from the British Library

ISBN: 9781032395968 (hbk)
ISBN: 9781032395951 (pbk)
ISBN: 9781003350477 (ebk)

DOI: 10.4324/9781003350477

Typeset in Univers LT Std
by Newgen Publishing UK

Access the Support Material: resourcecentre.routledge.com/speechmark

Contents

Foreword	ix
Preface	xiii
Acknowledgements	xv
Data availability statement	xvi
Part 1: About this book	**1**
About this resource	3
Aims of this resource	3
Who is this book for?	4
How to use this book	5
Terminology used	6
Theories underpinning this resource	6
A model for improving outcomes	8
Part 2: An introduction to autism	**11**
A brief history of autism	13
About autism	15
Common autistic traits	16
More about autism	20
Autistic females	21
Part 3: Mainstream school and educational experiences for autistic females	**27**
Introduction	29
Learning	30
Communication	43
Social media	53
Social times	55
Friendships	58
Sensory issues	60
Meltdowns and shutdowns	63
Intense interests	66
Feelings and emotions	68
Anxiety and absence from school	72
Selective mutism	74
Self-esteem and masking	76
Transition	82
Puberty, gender and sexuality	85
Interpreting the world	89
Final thoughts	96

Part 4: Practical resources — **101**

    School, staff and environmental audits — 103

    Self-awareness — 122

    Learning — 131

    Transitions and moving on — 145

    Anxiety and wellbeing — 157

Further reading and resources — 167

Index — 171

Foreword

Over the last eight years, our understanding of autistic girls and the challenges they experience at school and home has greatly increased from autobiographies, social media, clinical experience and research. The second edition combines that new knowledge to provide explanations and guidance for teachers, health professionals and parents.

We currently acknowledge that autism occurs in one in 44 children, and recent research on the gender ratio indicates a male-to-female ratio of 4 to 1 for primary school-age children, 3 to 1 for secondary-age children and 2 to 1 for adults. This means that many autistic girls are not diagnosed during their early school years and that every primary and secondary school will have several autistic girls.

What are the early signs of autism in girls? Parents may notice that their daughter does not play reciprocally with other young girls. She is often perceived as taking control of the play and being 'bossy', showing great distress if the rules of the game are changed or 'broken'. She may consider the play of other girls as boring or incomprehensible and clearly prefers to play in solitude so that she can do things her own way without interruption, and according to her own expectations and plans. She is alone but not feeling lonely. Her play and intellectual interests can be different to other girls, not necessarily in terms of topic, but rather in terms of intensity, quality, attention to detail and memory. She may determinedly organise and arrange toys and objects, such as her collection of pebbles or pencils, rather than share them. She may also play with toys in unconventional ways. For example, she may collect Barbie dolls, yet choose not to enact with her friend's 'Barbie going shopping'. Instead, she may choose to arrange the dolls in particular configurations, such as clothing. She may prefer non-gender-specific toys, such as Lego, or playing with toys usually associated with boys, such as construction sets, dinosaurs and vehicles. She may also not be interested in appearing feminine; for example, she may choose not to wear the latest fashions or brightly coloured or patterned clothing. Her preference may be for practical, comfortable clothes with lots of pockets. We have recently recognised that autistic girls may not have the range of movement disorders associated with autistic boys, and she may enjoy and excel at activities such as dancing, ice skating, athletics and team sports.

She may also not seek acquisitions related to the latest craze for girls her age to be included in their play. Autistic girls often develop talents in the arts, such as drawing, music and singing, and her social confusion may be overlooked as people admire and applaud her artistic abilities.

Autistic girls are different to autistic boys, not in terms of the central characteristics of autism but in terms of their reaction to being different. Autism is associated with the ability to determine patterns and systems, which can be applied to learning social rules and conventions. An autistic girl may avidly observe her peers to know what to do by intellect rather than intuition. This constructive strategy facilitates social engagement and inclusion. However, if the social rules seem elusive, autistic girls can effectively camouflage or mask their confusion in social situations by imitation, effectively 'acting' in social situations. They observe and replay popular girls' body language, interests and script, creating an alternative persona. They become social 'chameleons'. To do this, they must suppress their autistic characteristics and 'act' like their peers. The quality of acting can be so good that a teacher may not recognise autism and consider the girl too social to be autistic. This strategy of camouflaging or masking autism has the secondary benefit of reducing the likelihood of being bullied and socially rejected. However, socialising is a source of 'performance' anxiety, stress and mental exhaustion. She has surface sociability but a lack of authentic social identity.

Another adaptation to autism is avoiding social interactions by escaping into an alternative world of fantasy, engaging in creative and imaginative play, avidly reading and writing fiction, or spending enjoyable time interacting with pets and animals. Her friend may be a fellow artist, and they sit together quietly at lunchtime, drawing anime and manga together at school. Another adaptation is to seek the company of boys whose social play is active and more straightforward than that of girls whose play relies more on conversation, social hierarchies and the ability to read subtle social cues. They can be very intolerant of someone who is not an expert in social dynamics and nuances such as rolling eyes. Boys engage in more constructive, adventurous and more straightforward play activities and conversations. An autistic girl may develop talents in school subjects that are popular with boys, such as mathematics and science. She may also appear to understand the male, rather than the female, mind in terms of socialising, thinking, humour and priorities.

The early childhood signs of autism in girls can include intense emotions, especially anxiety, agitation and distress, an inability to be comforted by affection, or the intense feelings alleviated by distraction and compassion. Parents are aware of a propensity at home to have a meltdown, and meltdowns can eventually occur at school. Another sign in early childhood is sensory sensitivity, mainly auditory and tactile sensitivity. It is essential to recognise and address sensory sensitivity at school.

Other early signs of autism include difficulty coping with change, transitions and the unexpected such as a surprise test and resistance to a change in the classroom and household routines. There can also be an unusual language profile, such that, while the acquisition of speech may not be delayed, the linguistic profile can include problems with the pragmatic aspects of language – the 'art of conversation' and making a literal interpretation. There is also a tendency to be pedantic and sometimes unusual prosody or an unexpected accent, for example, the accent of characters in a favourite television programme.

If an autistic girl does have friendships, they are likely to be quite intense and exclusive, usually with one preferred girl rather than a small group of girls. This single friend may guide her in social situations, effectively becoming a teacher aide in the classroom or playground. In return, the autistic girl is a loyal and helpful friend, rarely interested in the critical and divisive behaviour of her female peers. Her friend feels safe.

Those autistic adolescent girls who mask their autism recognise that their female peers are increasingly interested in fashion and makeup. They may then develop expertise in fashion and makeup to be popular with their adolescent peers. Their interest in fashion means they create a 'costume' to accompany their social performance.

During adolescence, most autistic girls are renowned at school for being extraordinarily well-behaved and reminding their peers of the school rules and moral codes. They are considered social exemplars by teachers. A feeling that their peers may not reciprocate. However, some adolescent autistic girls recognise that they may never be accepted by their peers, no matter how hard they try. They have poor self-identity, based on peer criticisms and rejection, rather than on compliments and inclusion. They decide that, rather than enforce social and moral conventions; they will deliberately contravene them and despise femininity and conventional female roles. If they cannot connect with the popular girls, they may associate with marginalised peers. They have a yearning for connection and may be drawn to groups of secondary school students with a broader tolerance of being different such as those exploring drugs, gender identity and eating disorders. Due to their social naivety, they are also vulnerable to friendship predators or 'frenemies' and sexual predators; they lack the intuitive ability to identify those whose intentions are not honourable and make superficial judgements based on what someone says than their intentions or notoriety. Autistic girls may not have a close friend who can warn them, and schools need to be aware of this characteristic and provide guidance.

Over the last eight years, there has been considerable research on the association between autism and gender dysphoria and eating disorders. Autistic girls will have recognised that they are different to their peers from an early age and will have subjectively explored that difference. They can become natural philosophers and psychologists and engage in solitary self-analysis at a deeper and broader level than their peers. This can include aspects of existentialism and questioning gender identity, and seeking information on the Internet and social media. This may start a connection with similar adolescents seeking an explanation of why they are different. The despair of being different and a lack of connection with peers can contribute to the development of clinical depression. We recognise that autistic girls are more prone to develop depression and self-harm than their peers.

Autistic adolescents can experience a 'tsunami' of anxiety with the onset of puberty. Autistic adolescent girls may express their deep anxiety in many forms: generalised anxiety disorder;

performance anxiety, especially fear of failure or ridicule; phobias for specific situations, such as sensory experiences; social anxiety and situational mutism. High levels of anxiety are also associated with the development of eating disorders, and autistic girls are particularly vulnerable due to their aversion since early childhood to the sensory aspects of food.

There may also be the development of characteristics in the teenage years that appear consistent with a personality disorder. The challenges that an autistic girl experiences in social situations, especially the making and keeping of friends; knowing the appropriate level and intensity of behaviour within the friendship; and regulation of her emotions, particularly her tendency to catastrophise when a friendship ends – may lead to her being diagnosed with a borderline personality disorder.

Information from social media describes the concept of autistic burnout. The burnout is driven by the stress of masking and living in an autism-unfriendly environment, such as a school with limited knowledge and support mechanisms for autistic students. Mental and physical exhaustion, social withdrawal, executive functioning problems and increased autistic traits characterise burnout. Thus, autistic adolescent girls may need school support for various mental health issues and potential burnout.

It is becoming ever more critical to explore and describe the many ways in which teachers, psychologists, therapists and parents can help autistic girls during their school years, especially in the areas of accommodating aspects of autism such as sensory sensitivity, a different learning style, social inclusion and being the authentic self. This excellent, now-revised resource by Victoria Honeybourne goes a long way to achieving that.

Tony Attwood

Clinical Psychologist
Associate Professor at Griffith University, Australia

March 2023

Preface

I'm very excited to share with you this second edition of *Educating and Supporting Autistic Girls*. When I wrote the first edition in 2015, there was still relatively little published about autistic girls and many autistic females were left undiagnosed, or misdiagnosed. Thankfully, there has been growing interest in this field over the past ten years or so and there is now far greater awareness and better understanding of how autism isn't 'just a boy thing'. Much more has been researched and written about autistic females over the past decade, with a greater proportion of it produced – yay! – by autistic writers and researchers themselves. We now have much more insight into life from autistic perspectives, and there is now greater acceptance that there is no one way to 'be' autistic. Autism can present in many different ways, whatever your gender identity.

Understanding of autism in general has also evolved greatly over the past few years. In the preface to my first edition, I wrote that 'in my ideal world ... neurodiversity would simply be accepted and celebrated'. Although that's unfortunately still some way off, I do believe some huge strides have been made recently, with a growing awareness and understanding of neurodiversity in education, the workplace and public services. It's generally more accepted that neurodiversity not only exists, but also that neurodivergent individuals are disadvantaged because of the neurotypically designed society we live in, rather than because there is something inherently 'wrong' with how their brains work. There is still much work to be done in changing societal attitudes and expectations, but the process has begun.

Taking a wider perspective, global events of the past few years have accelerated change. The COVID pandemic and Black Lives Matters (BLM) movement, for example, both brought to the front some major structural societal inequalities which still exist today. Many people have become properly aware, for the first time, of the hidden difficulties and institutionalised discrimination that marginalised groups experience on a daily basis. It's positive to see greater representation and visibility of minority groups in the mainstream media compared with even just a few years ago. This includes greater visibility of autistic individuals, especially those with 'less typical' presentations. There are openly autistic female television celebrities, best-selling young adult novels with autistic protagonists written by autistic authors, and television shows with autistic main characters played by autistic actors.

Despite these steps forward, there is still a lot to be done. Many autistic children and young people continue to struggle in school settings with their needs not being adequately recognised or met. Waiting lists for assessments and diagnoses continue to lengthen and national lockdowns left many young people unable to access the support they needed. Many autistic adults continue to face difficulties in gaining and maintaining employment, as well as facing discrimination in other aspects of life. Funding services and support are an additional issue in these times of the cost-of-living crisis.

All these factors have led to me wanting to update this book. Since writing the first edition, I've also become aware of topics that require more space – such as the impact of social media on autistic girls, how greatly anxiety affects autistic individuals, and how changes relating to puberty can affect autistic girls differently than their neurotypical peers. New topics have been included here, and other topics expanded upon. Even the terminology used has changed enormously over the past decade. The term 'Asperger Syndrome' has largely been phased out and some of the language used in the first edition sounds outdated, even just eight years later! The way we talk about neurodiversity is changing as attitudes change – I apologise now if the updated language in this edition starts to sound dated in another few years' time!

Finally, my personal understanding of neurodiversity, and of my own autism, has also changed significantly since I originally set pen to paper to write the first edition. At that time, I had only been diagnosed a few years myself. Since then, I've held a number of different roles professionally within the education sector, written books on neurodiversity and had many personal experiences which have caused me to reflect further on how everyday situations and common attitudes affect those who are 'different'. I've become more aware of both my own internalised ableism, and institutional ableism that creates barriers to implementing change in educational and other settings.

There's, therefore, a slight change of emphasis in this edition. There are still the invaluable insights from a wonderful group of autistic girls and young women who share their experiences (thank you to everyone who contributed once again!), there are still tips and strategies as to how environments and communication in education settings can be made more autism-friendly, there are still activities to help autistic girls gain self-awareness, self-confidence and empowerment. The difference is that I hope to bring increased attention to how organisations, policies, practices, systems and unconscious biases discriminate against neurodivergent students.

I hope you find this updated edition useful and I hope it goes some way towards helping to make education and other settings more inclusive and accepting of neurodivergent students.

Victoria Honeybourne

Neurodiversity trainer and writer

February 2023

Acknowledgements

I would like to thank the many autistic females who have shared their experiences, thoughts and feelings with me during my research for this book (and my earlier first edition). A huge thank you for your contributions to this resource which will hopefully lead to greater understanding of autistic experiences among professionals and improved outcomes for autistic students in the future.

I would also like to thank the Society of Authors for awarding me a World of Books Impact Award which helped immensely with the writing of this second edition.

Data availability statement

Data not available due to ethical reasons. Due to the nature of this research, participants who contributed to Part 3 of this book did not agree for their data to be shared publicly, so supporting data are not available.

Part 1
About this book

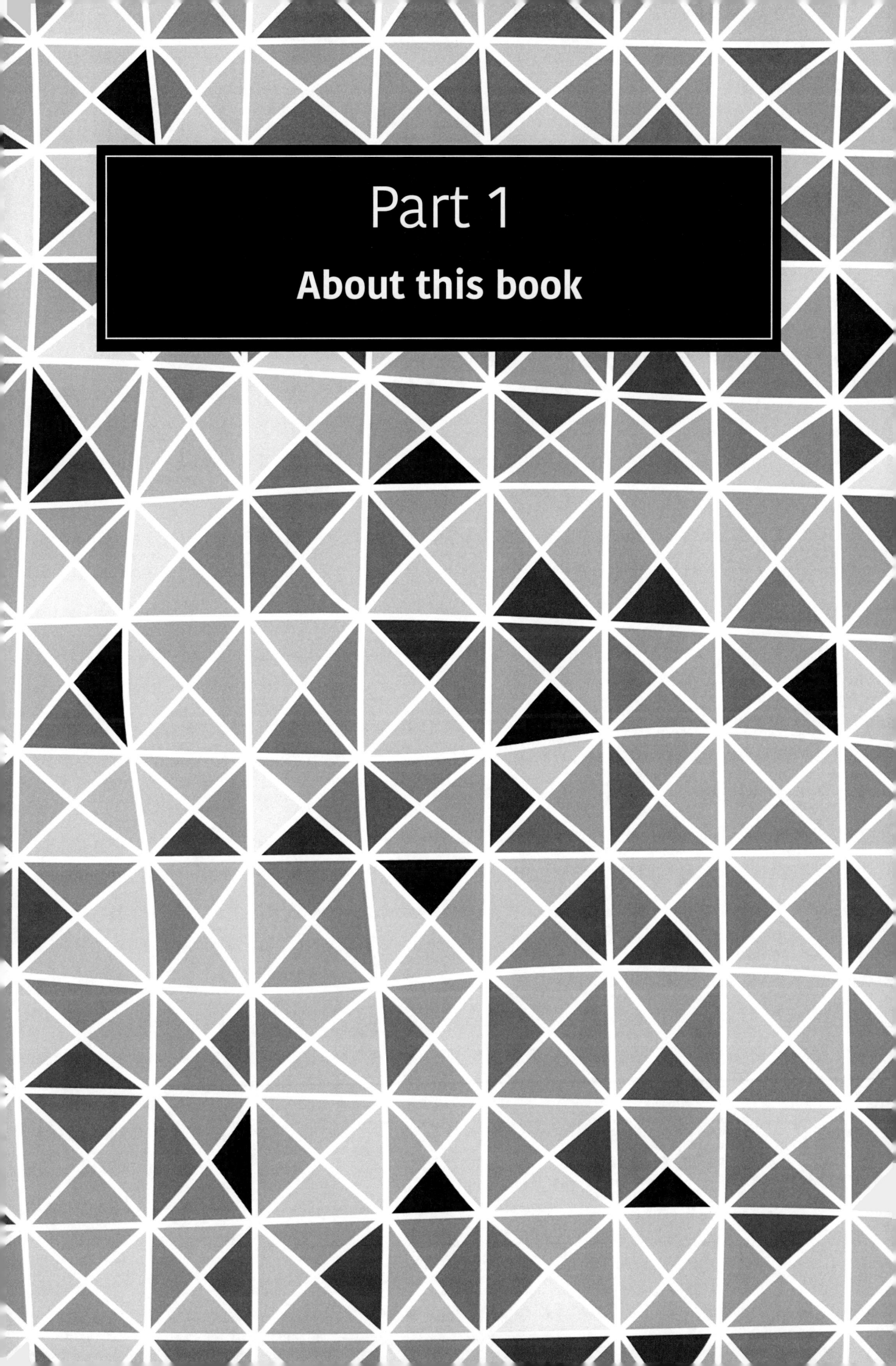

About this resource

Welcome to the second edition of *Educating and Supporting Autistic Girls*. It is now widely recognised that autism in girls has frequently been overlooked, missed or misdiagnosed for a variety of reasons. Professionals and diagnosticians have become aware that autistic girls (and some autistic boys) may present very differently than traditionally expected and therefore have different needs.

It needs to be made clear at the outset, however, that it's not quite as simple as saying 'all autistic girls are like this, and all autistic boys are like that'. There are many traits autistic individuals of all genders will have in common. There are also autistic girls who fit the more traditional 'male' profile of autism, autistic boys who fit the more 'female' profile, and a huge range of other experiences. Of course, gender can't simply be classified into the two categories of male and female either. There are other gender identities too (such as being non-binary, gender-neutral or gender-fluid).

Understanding of autism is evolving constantly. Traditionally, autism research and diagnostic criteria were based almost exclusively on the experience of white cisgender boys and it was believed autism was 'just a boy thing'. Then came the awareness that girls were affected too but that autism often presented differently in females. And now there's greater recognition that autism can present in many different ways, and affects people of all genders, sexualities, colours, ethnicities and socio-economic backgrounds. This book investigates the experiences of autistic girls in detail, as this is an area that was missed in the research literature for many years and is a group that still often goes misdiagnosed, but most of the strategies and suggestions are equally valid for autistic students of any gender. Many of the strategies can also be helpful for other groups of neurodivergent students (and indeed, neurotypical students) who share some similar differences and difficulties in educational settings.

Aims of this resource

The aims of this resource are:

- To help readers gain a greater insight into the lives, strengths, experiences and perspectives of autistic girls and young women
- To support professionals to understand and adopt the neurodiversity paradigm in their work
- To support professionals working with autistic students to create more inclusive and autism-friendly environments and to communicate in more inclusive ways
- To support professionals with resources and activities to use when working with autistic students
- To support autistic students to gain greater self-awareness and to help them achieve during their educational careers and beyond

Who is this book for?

This book is predominantly written for health and education professionals. Some people who might find it useful are:

- SENCOs/AENCOs (Special/Additional Educational Needs Co-ordinators)
- Teachers and Trainee Teachers
- Teaching/Learning Support Assistants
- Specialist/Outreach Teachers
- Pastoral Staff
- School Counsellors
- Mental Health Workers and Therapists
- Youth Workers
- Speech and Language Therapists
- Social Workers and Family Support Workers
- Educational Welfare Officers
- Disability Officers in Further and Higher Education
- Support Workers and Advocates
- Parents and Carers of Autistic Students

Many of the general strategies and environmental changes suggested in this book are suitable for all age groups of students. For example, getting the physical environment and adult communication right is important for autistic students whether in early years education, school settings or higher education institutions, although, obviously, specifics will change depending on the age group you are working with.

The worksheets and activities are designed for roughly the 9–19 age range, although some can be adapted for younger or older students who would benefit. Some resources focus on a specific age range (such as the transition from primary to secondary school). The 9–19 age range has been chosen as girls are often diagnosed as autistic later than their male counterparts (Idring et al., 2012). Many first become more aware of their difficulties around the time of puberty and the transition to secondary school, which often coincides with the time that the focus of friendships change and young people begin to become more aware of their individual differences. It is always important to keep in mind that every student is different, so individual students might be ready to engage with different activities at different ages.

The resources are aimed mainly at students educated in mainstream settings, although some will also be useful for students in specialist settings. The research project that fed into the creation of this book came from respondents who – mainly – had been educated in mainstream schools. My professional experience has also been working in mainstream settings. Therefore, while not intending to ignore or marginalise any group, it is outside the scope of this book to cover in detail how best to support autistic students who also have more complex learning and communication needs and co-occurring disabilities. There are other books which cover those topics far more comprehensively and some of those are listed in the Further Reading and Resources section.

How to use this book

Part 2 of this book is a brief introduction to autism. It covers general topics such as diagnosis, common autistic traits, difficulties autistic individuals face, current trends and research in the area, and specific differences that autistic females can experience. You might like to start here if you're new to autism or want a general refresher of the topic.

Part 3 covers educational experiences for autistic females in more detail. Many autistic girls and young women have contributed their thoughts, experiences and insights. Each sub-section finishes with some general tips and strategies for professionals.

Part 4 comprises worksheets, activities and resources for use with autistic students as well as staff and environmental audits. These do not have to be used in any particular order, although some do build on previous activities. Not all resources will be suitable for all students and some might need to be adapted for individual students. There is no 'right' way to complete any activity – drawing, discussion, role play or any other means of expression is equally as relevant as writing things down. Students might prefer to complete activities in different ways. Some might like to share what they have done, others might prefer to work through things independently. There are no 'right' answers. It will be repeated many times throughout this book, but every autistic student really is an individual! What one student might dislike, another will like, what one might find difficult, another will find easy, what is useful for one, might not be useful for another. The best advice is to get to know the individuals you work with – choose the activities that the individual needs, at the time that they need it.

> **Important!** Please note that the activities for autistic students in this book are designed simply as a guide to promote self-awareness and understanding in various areas. They are not designed as a substitute for professional mental health support. Students who need more extensive support should be referred to a relevant professional.

Terminology used

The terminology used to describe autism can be a hotly debated issue. Medical professionals tend still use the official diagnostic term 'Autism Spectrum Disorder (ASD)', however, many autistic people – myself included – argue against this, as they don't believe autism should be considered an illness, disorder or impairment, simply as a different – equally valid – way of being.

Some studies suggest that most autistic people prefer identity-first language (*autistic girls*) rather than person-first language (*girls with autism*) as they see their autism as an integral part of their whole being, not as something that can be separated from them (Kenny et al., 2015). Some individuals prefer terms such as 'on the autism spectrum' or 'autism spectrum conditions'.

Autism has been labelled differently at different points in time. *Asperger Syndrome* was the official term given to autistic people without co-occurring learning difficulties until 2013. Since then, individuals with that profile have been given a diagnosis of '*Autism (Level 1)*', rather than Asperger Syndrome. Some people still describe themselves as having Asperger Syndrome, as this was the label they were diagnosed with and have grown up with. The terms *High Functioning Autism* (HFA) and *Low Functioning Autism* (LFA) were also commonly used in the past, although such functioning labels are now widely rejected by the autism community, as these labels can hide the uneven profiles of individuals who might be very able in some areas but experience difficulties in others.

Many autistic individuals currently prefer to describe themselves as 'neurodivergent' – a term used to cover ways of being such as autism, ADHD, dyslexia and dyspraxia. Although these conditions have their differences, there can be some overlap and many of these groups share some of the same difficulties that arise from living in a society designed only for neurotypicals.

How autism and neurodiversity are described is constantly changing and will probably continue to change as attitudes and knowledge evolves.

In this book, I use identity-first language, except when quoting verbatim from other sources. I have also kept the original terminology from the girls and young women who I interviewed, in order to reflect their individual preferences in how they choose to describe themselves.

Theories underpinning this resource

This resource isn't about 'fixing' autism, but simply sees autism as a different, equally valid, way of being. The focus is on helping readers to gain a deeper understanding and acceptance of autism, while also supporting autistic students to gain self-awareness and self-acceptance. The aim is to help educators and other professionals to identify some of the barriers that exist in preventing autistic individuals from fulfilling their potential and to empower autistic students to feel happy in their own skin, rather than having to pretend to be somebody they are not.

This resource is based upon:

The neurodiversity paradigm

Neurodiversity (neurological diversity) is a term thought to have been first coined in the 1990s and simply means that there is a range of ways in which human brains function. In other words, our brains do not all process information in the same way, but rather we think, learn, process information and relate to others in different ways.

The neurodiversity paradigm considers diversity and differences in how brains function to be a totally natural and normal aspect of human variation. There is no 'right' or 'normal' way of being and no one group is superior to any other. It is normal to be different. From this perspective, educators, employers and society in general should accept *and expect* that a significant proportion of the population are neurodivergent – and should recognise that the systems currently in place have been designed only for the neurotypical population. This book encourages professionals to identify where policies, practices and environments could be disadvantaging neurodivergent students.

> ***Neurotypical (NT)*** – Having a style of neurocognitive functioning that falls within the current societal classification of 'normal'.
>
> ***Neurodivergent (ND)*** – Having a style of neurocognitive functioning which falls outside this idea of 'normal'. Individuals with diagnoses of conditions such as autism, dyslexia, dyspraxia, dyscalculia and ADHD are considered neurodivergent.

'When you've met one person with autism, you've met one person with autism'

This is an oft-repeated saying within the autism community, but one that is worth repeating again. Although autistic individuals share many traits and experiences, it should be remembered that the autism spectrum covers a wide range of abilities and differences and every individual has a different profile of strengths, differences, difficulties, support needs and life experiences (as you will see from the range of young women who share their stories in Part 3).

Therefore, not every section of this book will be relevant to every individual. Many of the resources and activities are open-ended and can be completed in a variety of ways depending on the individual. Just as not every neurotypical student will need or like the same things, nor will every neurodivergent student. It is important not to make assumptions about what autistic students can or can't do.

Person-centred approaches

This resource is based on person-centred approaches, which developed out of the work of Dr Carl Rogers (1902–87), and which move away from the concept of the professional being the expert and towards viewing the client as the expert on themselves (The Person Centred Association, 2020). Although originally developed as an approach to therapy, person-centred approaches have been transferred to settings such as childcare, teaching and management. Person-centred approaches look at the world from the individual's perspective, seeing what is important to them. This has particular relevance to autistic individuals who process and interpret the world differently to their neurotypical counterparts and their preferences should be given equal value to more neurotypical priorities.

Positive psychology

This resource also uses some ideas and strategies from the field of positive psychology. Positive psychology is described as 'the scientific study of human strengths and emotions'; and seeks to promote wellbeing, rather than to remediate deficits. The movement is based on the work of Martin Seligman who proposes that happiness, meaning and lasting fulfilment can be cultivated. The positive psychology movement also seeks to help people acquire the skills to be able to deal with everyday life in more positive ways (Seligman, 2002).

In the field of autism, more attention has traditionally been paid to the negative aspects of the condition and to finding a cure rather than to the positives and to how to increase the wellbeing and happiness of autistic people (Vermeulen, 2014). More than half of all research and funding on autism in the UK, for example, is spent on investigating the biological causes of autism (Pellicano et al., 2014). This book uses some of the strategies from the positive psychology movement in order to support autistic students to learn techniques to support their wellbeing.

A model for improving outcomes

In order to improve outcomes for autistic students, I believe the following four things are needed. The resources in this book are based on these ideas.

Acceptance: By far the most important aspect is acceptance, both from others and self-acceptance. Policy-makers, educators, health and care professionals, employers and society in general need to become more aware of and accepting of neurodiversity, realising that different does not mean inferior or wrong, just different – and that this diversity in how brains work is a totally normal and natural aspect of human variation. Self-acceptance for neurodivergent individuals is also vital (as it is for others too!) – accepting that your own way of being is as equally valid as anybody else's and feeling confident enough to be yourself.

Environmental changes: It also needs to be recognised that our physical environments, which includes the systems, policies and practices in place in these environments, have been designed predominantly for the neurotypical brain and this puts neurodivergent individuals at a real disadvantage. In the education sector, for example, simple changes to the physical environment, how adults communicate, and school policies, can make a huge difference to neurodivergent students.

Self-awareness: Increasing self-awareness can be helpful for autistic individuals as it can contribute to increased wellbeing and help them make more informed decisions. Having self-awareness is also a key aspect of being able to develop positive coping strategies. Society isn't yet designed for neurodivergent individuals and some might benefit from developing 'coping strategies' for certain situations. A positive coping strategy can be things as simple as wearing earplugs to block out noise in a busy waiting room, asking to work in a quieter room, or deciding to leave a social event early if the individual feels they have reached their social limit. It can also be important to identify any unhelpful coping strategies which might in fact contribute to increased anxiety or low self-esteem.

Direct teaching and learning: Some neurodivergent students might benefit from being taught some skills more directly. For example, some can benefit from learning organisational skills, study skills, independent living skills or strategies to improve their wellbeing. This isn't the same as teaching a student to be 'less autistic' or to change themselves to fit in with neurotypical expectations (neither of which is helpful and will likely only cause increased difficulties) but can give autistic students practical skills to enable them to achieve and empower them.

Key points

- There has traditionally been less written about the subtler presentation of autism, often more commonly associated with females.
- Autistic girls can present differently than autistic boys in school settings, although they will share some of the same traits, and there can be a wide range of experiences.
- Many of the strategies relating to adult communication and environmental changes are relevant for a wide range of settings – from schools to youth clubs, health and social care settings and the home.

- The resources and ideas in this book will not all be relevant for every student, do not have to be worked through in a certain order and can be completed in any way the student prefers. Getting to know individual students is key to improving outcomes.
- This book takes the view that neurodiversity is a natural aspect of human variation and different ways of being, such as autism, should be accepted and expected, not seen as inferior.

References

Idring S., Rai D., Dal H., Dalman C., Sturm H., Zander E., Lee B.K., Serlachius E. & Magnusson C. (2012) Autism spectrum disorders in the Stockholm Youth Cohort: design, prevalence and validity. *PLOS ONE*, 7 (7), e41280.

Kenny L., Hattersley C., Mollins B., Buckley C., Povey C. & Pellicano L. (2015) Which terms should be used to describe autism? Perspectives from the UK autism community. *Autism Journal*, 20, Issue 4.

Pellicano L., Dinsmore A. & Charman D. (2014) *A Future Made Together: Shaping Autism Research in the UK.* Centre for Research in Autism and Education (CRAE), London.

Seligman M. (2002) *Authentic Happiness.* Free Press: New York.

The Person-Centred Association (2020), online, *What is the person-centred approach?* (the-pca.org.uk) [accessed 29 June 2022].

Vermeulen P. (2014) The practice of promoting happiness in autism. *Good Autism Practice: Autism, Wellbeing and Happiness.* University of Birmingham, Birmingham, UK.

Part 2
An introduction to autism

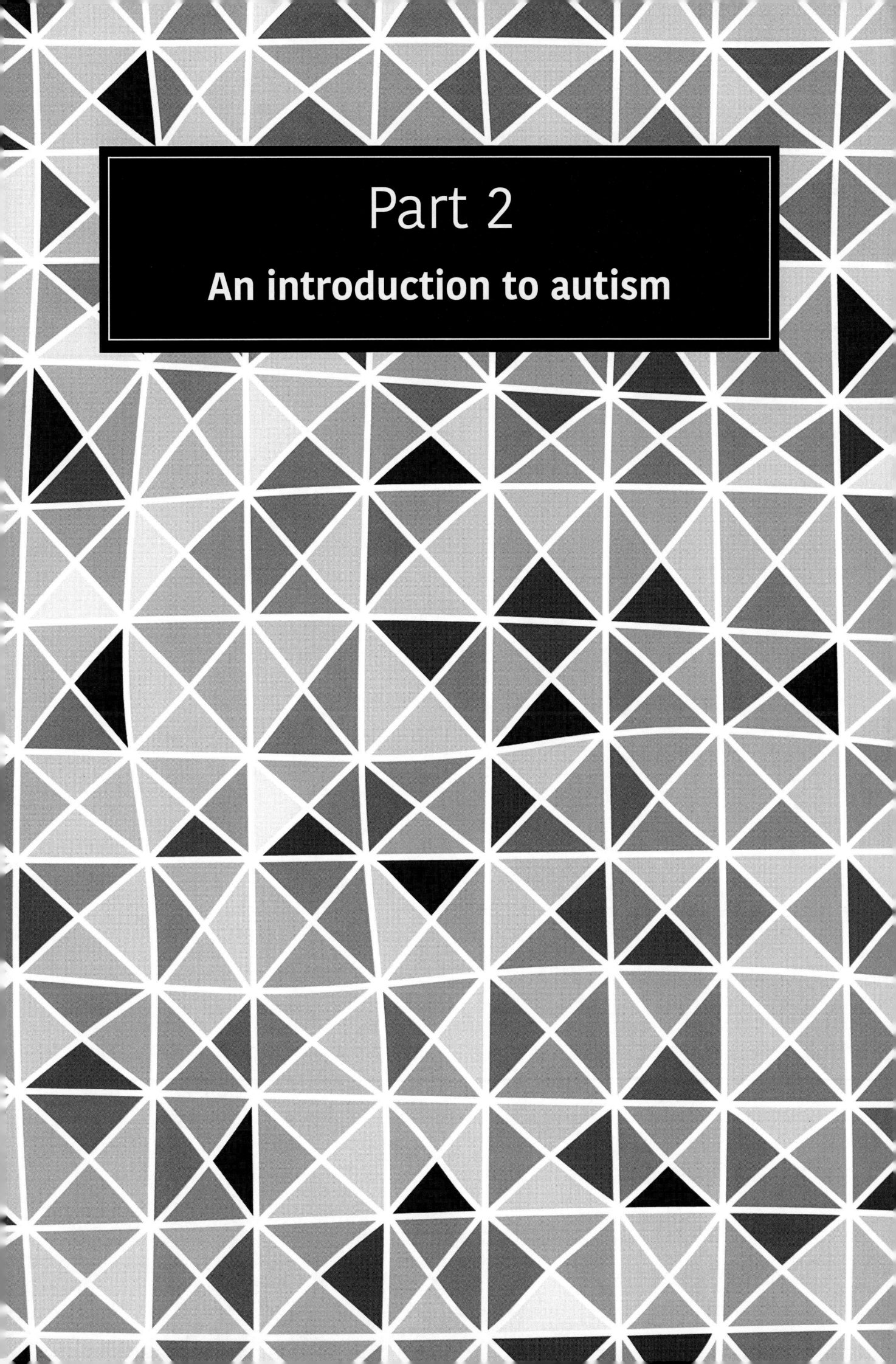

A brief history of autism

When was autism first named?

Well, autistic people have likely been around for as long as anybody else, but it was only in the 1940s that this way of being was first given a name. The American child psychiatrist, Dr Leo Kanner, was one of the first to describe autism in a group of children he was working with. These children with learning difficulties were socially isolated and showed little interest in interacting with others. This form of autism then went on to be called 'classic autism' or 'Kanner's autism'. The word autism has Greek origins with 'autos' meaning 'self'. This reflected the idea that these children often seemed very self-contained and had difficulties interacting with others.

Around the same time, Austrian Dr Hans Asperger was also identifying a group of children he called 'autistic'. These children did not have learning difficulties, and this form of autism went on to be called 'Asperger Syndrome'.

And what happened next?

By the 1980s, British psychiatrist Lorna Wing had proposed the idea of an autism 'spectrum', recognising that there was a huge range of ways in which individuals were affected by autism. Lorna Wing was also one of the first to recognise that almost 15 times as many men were diagnosed with high-functioning autism (as it was called at the time) than women, although that ratio was closer to 2:1 in autistic people with learning difficulties. Lorna Wing (1981) also identified a 'triad of impairments' which affected autistic people: difficulties in the areas of social communication, social interaction and social imagination.

Many different 'types' of autism also came to be identified, such as classic autism, Asperger Syndrome, high-functioning autism (another term used to describe autistic people without learning difficulties), childhood disintegrative disorder, PDD-NOS (Pervasive Developmental Disorder–Not Otherwise Specified) and Pathological Demand Avoidance (PDA).

> **Functioning labels**
>
> Many people don't find functioning labels helpful. Just because an autistic person might be of average or above average intelligence (and therefore considered 'high functioning'), doesn't mean they function at a high level in all areas of life, or at all times.

Where are we now?

Definitions of autism have changed over the years and are likely to change again as understanding evolves. Terms such as Asperger Syndrome, childhood disintegrative disorder and

PDD-NOS have been replaced in the latest diagnostic manuals and the collective term 'autism spectrum disorder' is now used to cover all these categories. It is also worth noting that a paper published in 2018 suggested that Dr Hans Asperger might have had some links with the Nazi Party (Czech, 2018) – another reason why some people prefer no longer to use the term Asperger Syndrome.

Autism is a lifelong difference in how people interpret, experience and interact with the world around them. Some people describe it as their brains working on a 'different operating system' to others, or seeming to be 'on a different wavelength'.

An 'official' definition of autism, taken from the DSM-5 Manual, which is used by psychiatrists to diagnose, describes autism as 'persistent difficulties with social communication and social interaction' and 'restricted and repetitive patterns of behaviours, activities or interests' (this includes sensory behaviours), present since early childhood, to the extent that these 'limit and impair everyday functioning' (DSM-5-TR, 2022).

Pathological Demand Avoidance (PDA)

Pathological Demand Avoidance is now widely recognised as a profile on the autism spectrum (PDA Society, 2023). A PDA profile of autism means that individuals share autism characteristics (such as the difficulties with social communication and interaction and sensory differences) and in addition: resist and avoid everyday demands of life; use social strategies as part of the avoidance; might appear 'socially able' although this can mask underlying difficulties; appear comfortable in role play and pretence; have an intense focus, often on other people; and have an extreme need for control driven by anxiety (PDA Society, 2023). Understanding of the PDA profile is constantly evolving, just as with other autism profiles.

Conventional teaching, parenting and support approaches tend to be less successful with PDA individuals. An approach that is based on trust, flexibility, collaboration, careful use of language and balancing demands often works best (PDA Society, 2023). Although some approaches suggested in this book might be beneficial for PDA individuals – such as the importance of getting the environment right and changing attitudes, this book does not cover PDA in detail. The 'Further Reading and Resources' section suggests where more information on PDA can be found.

About autism

So is autism an illness, a disease, a mental health difficulty, a disability or what?

Autism isn't a disease or a mental illness. Understanding of the brain and mind has developed a great deal over recent decades, and it is now generally recognised that autism is a lifelong neurodevelopmental condition (like ADHD or dyslexia). Let's go back in time a bit to investigate…

It's only fairly recently in human history that we've started to understand more about how the human brain and mind work. For thousands of years, the 'moral diagnosis' was the prevailing paradigm (Hallowell & Ratey, 2005) – any sort of mental illness (and autistic-type difficulties would have been considered this in the past) was seen as a failure of will, a result of weak character, a curse, an outright sin, attention-seeking behaviour, or some other fault of the individual. People with an 'invisible' difference, difficulty or disability would have been told that they were being lazy or just needed to try harder. In other times and places, they'd have been told they were possessed by the devil or some other demon or curse. Even though modern science has given us much greater insight into the human mind, this moral thinking still hasn't disappeared altogether – there is a stigma about mental health conditions, particularly in some cultures and traditions.

As doctors became more eminent within society, the medical model of disability came to the fore. This model suggests that there is something wrong within the individual which needs to be fixed, cured or treated. Within this model an individual's deficits are labelled and described using clinical terminology (Skidmore, 1996) and individuals are judged against developmental and functional norms of others their age (Hodkinson, 2016). The medical model still prevails in many health systems and societies today. Individuals are labelled with a condition and given some sort of medication, treatment or intervention to help them become 'more normal'. Autistic people in the past, for example, might have been prescribed behavioural treatments that rewarded 'normal' behaviours and punished 'autistic' behaviours.

Late in the 20th century, the social model of disability gained prominence. This started to consider that it is the environments, attitudes, values and beliefs operating within a society which cause individuals to be 'disabled'; it is society that needs to be treated and cured, not individuals (Johnstone, 2001). So, in relation to autism, for example, this model of disability proposes that it is the environments and expectations of others that cause problems, rather than being autistic in itself. Over the past decades, this social model of disability has become more accepted and embedded in many aspects of society – although there is still some way to go.

Neurodiversity (neurological diversity) is a term thought to have been first coined in the 1990s and simply means that there is a range of ways in which human brains function. In other words, our brains do not all process information in the same way, but rather we think, learn, process information and relate to others in different ways.

Until recently, this diversity in how brains work was not recognised. It was believed there was one 'right' way of functioning (the neurotypical way) and anybody whose brain did not work in this way must be 'abnormal', 'disordered', 'ill' or somehow inferior. These individuals were – and still are – given labels such as autism, attention deficit hyperactivity disorder (ADHD), dyslexia and dyspraxia. The emphasis was, until recently, on fixing these individuals to help them be more 'normal'.

The neurodiversity paradigm is a perspective which follows the social model of disability. The neurodiversity paradigm (which this book promotes) considers diversity and differences in how brains function to be a totally natural and normal aspect of human variation. There is no 'right' or 'normal' way of being and no one group is superior to any other. It is normal to be different. From this perspective, educators, employers and society in general should accept and expect that a significant proportion of the population are neurodivergent – and should recognise that the systems currently in place have been designed only for the neurotypical population.

Common autistic traits

Ah ok. Right, but what are autistic people actually like? They're all like that guy in the Rain Man ***film, right? And that book about the boy who doesn't speak***

No, most aren't like that at all! The *Rain Man* character is autistic and has extraordinary 'savant' mathematical and memory abilities, but the vast majority of autistic people actually don't have those exceptional abilities. And yes, there are some autistic individuals who don't speak, but many others are very articulate indeed. Autism is viewed as a spectrum condition, meaning that it affects people in different ways. So, if you watch a film or read a book about an autistic person, the autistic people you meet in real life might be very different.

Hmmm… sounds confusing. So how come all these people with the same diagnosis are all so different?

Well, some people do argue that the autism spectrum is too broad and think that an autistic person with complex support needs and learning difficulties shouldn't be given the same label as an autistic individual who is highly intelligent and lives independently. Maybe definitions and categories will change again at some point in the future. However, all autistic people do share difficulties in the following areas (adapted from NAS, 2022):

Social communication and interaction

Some autistic people might have no or limited speech, while others have good language skills. Difficulties can include:

- Interpreting and using both verbal and non-verbal language (such as body language or tone of voice)
- Needing extra time to process language
- Taking things literally
- Repeating what others say
- Understanding others' feelings and intentions
- Recognising, understanding and expressing their own emotions
- Seeking 'alone' time when overwhelmed
- Not seeking comfort in expected ways
- Appearing to behave in a way that is 'strange' or socially 'inappropriate'
- Finding it hard to form and maintain friendships and relationships

Repetitive and restricted behaviours might include

- Finding the world confusing and unpredictable
- Needing routines so that they know what is going to happen (such as wearing the same clothes)
- Making repetitive movements (such as hand flapping or rocking)
- Finding it distressing to cope with change and unpredictability

In addition, most autistic people also experience:

Sensory differences

- Over- or under-sensitivity to light, noise, touch, taste, smell, colours, temperature or pain. Things like background music that others can block out, can be unbearably loud and painful for autistic people, for example.
- Finding everyday places such as schools, workplaces or shopping centres overwhelming and cause sensory overload

Highly focused hobbies or interests

- Interests might be usual (such as the environment or trains) or more unusual (like collecting bottle tops), but the intensity of the interest is what makes it different
- Some might become so engrossed in their interest that they neglect other aspects of life

Extreme anxiety

- Anxiety can be severe especially in social situations or when faced with change
- Many autistic people experience difficulty in identifying and managing their emotions

Shutdowns or meltdowns

- When an autistic person becomes completely overwhelmed with their current situation they can experience a meltdown, losing control verbally (shouting, crying, etc.), physically (kicking, lashing out, etc.) or both
- A shutdown appears less obvious to others (an autistic person going quiet or 'switching off') but can be equally debilitating
- These are not 'temper tantrums' but intense and frightening experiences when the sensory system becomes overwhelmed

Lists like these aren't always very useful, as they don't really explain what everyday life is like for an autistic individual, but they do highlight the main areas of difficulty that lead to a diagnosis of autism.

An autistic individual will usually have significant difficulties in most of these areas. The difficulties will need to impact negatively on daily life for an individual to receive a diagnosis. A person who scores highly on just one area might be more likely to be identified as experiencing something other than autism – a developmental language difficulty, for example, or a sensory processing disorder.

Hmmmm, ok, but that all sounds… rather negative. Are there no positives?

Unfortunately, lists like these do tend to focus on the negatives and difficulties, but autistic people, just like anybody else, also have just as many positive qualities and characteristics. Every individual will have specific skills and strengths and many autistic people do extremely well in their chosen fields. An extreme passion and in-depth knowledge of a special interest, for example, can lead to a fulfilling hobby or career – look at autistic climate campaigner, Greta Thunberg, for example, who uses her intense focus to such positive effect.

Other traits that some autistic people experience can include: an excellent memory and good ability to recall facts and figures; precision and attention to detail; honesty; persistence; loyalty; the ability not to be limited by social norms; intense focus; logical thinking; abilities to systemise and categorise information; thinking 'outside the box'; determination; and standing up for what they believe in.

Neurodivergent individuals simply have a different way of interpreting the world, rather than the 'wrong' way. Many difficulties arise from living in a world which is not designed for, or appreciates, their way of being. It's also now more recognised that neurodivergent individuals can bring a wide range of skills and abilities to the workplace and that a diverse workforce provides diversity of thought and results in increased creativity. Large organisations such as Microsoft, Ford, Google, SAP and DXC Technology all have recently run neurodiversity-at-work initiatives (CIPD, 2018) as they recognise neurodivergent individuals can bring innovative solutions and ideas but might have been excluded from such workplaces in the past. Organisations such as British spy agency GCHQ and weapons manufacturer BAE Systems also issued appeals recently for more neurodivergent women to apply to them for cybersecurity jobs (The Guardian, 2022), in particular roles that require 'fast pattern recognition, sharper accuracy and greater attention to detail'.

There is often a media stereotype that autistic people all want, and are suited to work, in IT but there are successful autistic people in all walks of life – there are successful autistic teachers, academics, authors, cleaners, gardeners, actors, musicians, therapists, and parents. There are autistic people who have strong relationships, good friendships, who contribute to their communities in a variety of ways, and who have a good level of wellbeing. Positive outcomes for autistic individuals are often a result of receiving the right support at the right time, being surrounded by supportive and understanding others and feeling confident and accepting of themselves.

Hey, a lot of these traits you mention affect lots of us. Is it true that we're all on the autism spectrum somewhere?

Well, lots of people share some of these traits, but we are certainly not all autistic. In fact, some people are calling for a move away from calling autism a spectrum condition, as it causes this sort of confusion. If we were all 'a bit autistic' then actually autistic people wouldn't experience all the difficulties, discrimination and misunderstandings that they do as there would be far more understanding from others! Yes, the traits mentioned above are all found in the general population. Anybody might experience things like social anxiety, difficulties communicating with others, sensory overwhelm and difficulties dealing with change from time to time (just think how frustrated you feel when your local supermarket swaps the aisles around, or when there is an unexpected diversion on the way to work). The difference for autistic people is the intensity and severity of these traits, and the impact on their lives.

Many neurodivergent people actually feel extremely misunderstood and dismissed when others say things like: 'oh, we're all a bit autistic', 'we're all on the spectrum somewhere' or 'I feel like that too'. Although these things are usually well-meant and the speaker is trying to show empathy, it can come across as the opposite and can show a lack of understanding and belief.

More about autism

Right, another question for you. How many people are actually autistic?

Well, figures differ, but current statistics from the National Autistic Society suggest that one in a hundred people are on the autism spectrum and that autism affects some 700,000 people in the UK (NAS, 2022). A 2018 report from the United States suggests that 1 in every 44 children is diagnosed on the autism spectrum (CDC, 2021). It's likely these numbers could be an under-estimate. Diagnostic services available can affect the numbers diagnosed. Figures also do not include those undiagnosed, misdiagnosed, those waiting for a diagnosis or who have chosen not to be diagnosed.

Autism occurs in people of all backgrounds, colours and identities, and might be under-identified in some communities. One 2014 report (NAS, 2014) suggests that there can be additional barriers to getting a diagnosis and support in some Black, Asian and Minority Ethnic (BAME) communities. In some cultures, disability is stigmatised more than in others, which can also affect the number of people seeking a diagnosis or support, and there can be a lack of awareness about autism in some communities.

I've heard people say there's an autism epidemic. It seems to be everywhere these days. Why are so many people getting a diagnosis? Is it spreading?

The number of people diagnosed as autistic has gone up over recent years but this is likely to be due to a range of factors. (It certainly isn't 'spreading'. You can't catch it like a cold!) Firstly, there is now far more awareness of the condition amongst health and education professionals and the general population. There is also growing recognition that previously many autistic individuals might have been 'missed' from the statistics, particularly females (we'll look at the reasons for this later), those with less typical presentations and those who don't have learning or language difficulties. Some people in the past may have been misdiagnosed with mental health issues or learning difficulties. There's also now less stigma attached to being autistic which might mean people are more likely to seek a diagnosis.

Ah, ok. But do people outgrow autism? Is that why there are fewer autistic adults about?

No, autism is a lifelong condition. It's present from childhood and it's not something you outgrow. You might not think there are not many autistic adults about, but in fact, there are lots!

It's important to remember that autism is an 'invisible disability', you can't tell that somebody is autistic just by looking at them. There are plenty of autistic adults out there but you might not know unless they choose to disclose this to you. Also, by the time some autistic people become adults, they have learned how to manage their differences and difficulties. They haven't outgrown their autism, but they've learned to work to their strengths and know how to reduce their sensory distress – therefore, more obvious meltdowns, shutdowns, anxiety and misunderstandings might reduce as they know the environments and situations to avoid.

Many autistic people report that they learn to 'mask' or to pretend to fit in, often by copying what others do and hiding their true identity. This can be exhausting and can lead to further anxiety, depression and low self-esteem, but it can be another reason why you don't 'see' their autism. And finally, neurodivergent individuals are, like other disabled people or minorities, a marginalised group, whose views are often ignored or dismissed in the mainstream media, which is why there doesn't seem to be so many of them. Thankfully, this is changing somewhat. There are more openly autistic individuals in high-profile roles, and more awareness in the media and other industries that diversity needs to be promoted.

And what causes autism?

It's not exactly known but is now thought to be genetic. There have been many theories put forward over the years which have proved to be untrue. For example, there is no strong evidence to show that autism is caused by emotional deprivation or the way a person has been brought up. There are also many studies that have investigated links between receiving childhood vaccines and developing autism. No link between the two has been found and the original research which suggested a link has now been discredited (Oxford Vaccine Group, 2020).

Is autism linked with any other difficulties?

Autism can occur with other difficulties and differences. Some autistic people have co-occurring learning difficulties and/or language difficulties. Other autistic individuals might also be diagnosed with other neurodivergent conditions such as dyslexia, ADHD, dyspraxia or dyscalculia.

There is evidence that autistic individuals are more likely than the general population to experience mental health difficulties such as depression, anxiety, eating disorders or post-traumatic stress disorder (MQ Mental Health Research, 2021).

Other difficulties should be properly assessed and investigated in autistic students and not simply put down to their autism. However, it's also important that other conditions are treated or managed taking into account a person's autism. Interventions which are successful in the neurotypical population might be more challenging for autistic individuals to engage with, unless their autism is taken into account.

Autistic females

Hang on a minute. This is a book about autism in girls, right? But everything you've mentioned so far is just as relevant to boys, isn't it?

Yes, so originally it was thought that autism was mainly a boy thing. This was because most of the participants in the original research back in the 1940s were boys. Far more males got a diagnosis of autism. Lorna Wing in the 1980s found that only one girl was diagnosed to every 15 boys. Media portrayals of autism also concentrated on men, and diagnostic criteria developed out of research which used mainly male participants.

It's only been much more recently that people have realised that just as many girls are autistic but that they present differently, often more subtly. (The same also goes for ADHD which was also considered 'just a boy thing' until recently.)

What has been found is that many autistic females often have a more subtle presentation of autism, rather than the more 'obvious' or 'visible' characteristics that were traditionally associated with autism. Of course, some autistic females have more obvious characteristics too, and some autistic males have the more subtle characteristics.

Ah, ok, so I see there might be some reasons why girls have been missed. Tell me more

So, let's see what researchers suggest about this more subtle presentation of autism:

- Autistic girls might be better at hiding their autism by using 'social mimicry skills'. They are perhaps more able to copy some expected behaviours than boys, so their autism isn't so obvious to observers.

- Autistic girls might cope in primary school as they might be 'mothered' by other girls and be more included and accepted by their peers. Difficulties might not become more apparent until secondary school when girls' relationships with each other can become more complicated (Hurley, 2014). This can delay identification and diagnosis.

- Autistic boys may be more likely to be bullied or may be more disruptive at school, which makes them more noticed (Hurley, 2014), whereas autistic girls might be more likely to internalise things and camouflage their difficulties (Solomon et al., 2012). Autistic males might be more likely to hit out aggressively or become bullies, whereas females may instead cling or over-attach to other females (Lawson, 2005). This perceived physical aggression again might bring these individuals to the attention of teachers and other professionals.

- Whereas autistic boys may have special interests which are technical and stand out from their peers, girls' interests may be similar to neurotypical peers (e.g. animals or celebrities). The difference is likely to be the intensity and dominance of these interests (Gould & Ashton-Smith, 2011). A girl might play with dolls, for example, but line these up in alphabetical order rather than initiating play with others (Attwood, 2007).

- Autistic girls may play with similar toys as their peers but in a different way. For example, autistic girls may follow a 'script' when playing with dolls and may not be able to predict the consequences of others (Gould & Ashton-Smith, 2011).

- Autistic girls might be more likely to hide their autism by using their intellectual abilities rather than intuition to determine what to say or to do (Attwood, 2007).

- Autistic girls might develop one intense friendship which reduces the likelihood of being identified as on the autism spectrum (Attwood, 2007; Gould & Ashton-Smith, 2011). Autistic girls might also be more motivated to socialise and might be better at making friends compared to autistic boys (Bargiela, 2019).
- Autistic females might be more open to talking about feelings and emotions and might be more expressive in gesture and facial expression than their male counterparts.
- Autistic girls may show less restricted repetitive and stereotyped patterns of behaviour (Van Wijngaarden et al., 2014), which can also make their autism harder to spot.

All these issues can contribute to why autistic females (and males who don't fit the conventional autism profile) might be missed – often they don't fit the stereotypical image of autism, can do a good job of hiding their difficulties, might be misdiagnosed with other conditions, or have their difficulties and differences dismissed because, on the surface, they are coping.

It's worth repeating again though, that it is not as clear cut as 'all autistic boys are like this and all autistic girls are like that'. There is a huge range of experiences, with some boys fitting the more 'female' profile and some girls fitting the more 'male' profile of autism. Gender identity doesn't simply divide into the two 'boy' and 'girl' categories either. It's perhaps best to understand there that autism can have a wider range of presentations than previously thought and that these can all apply to individuals of any gender.

What are the difficulties for autistic females?

Well, autistic individuals whose autism fits this more subtle presentation experience many of the same difficulties as those with more obvious characteristics. They have sensory sensitivities which can cause discomfort and distress, they can find it difficult to communicate with others and to develop friendships, they can experience intense anxiety, have intense interests and restricted, repetitive routines. However, there might also be additional difficulties:

- Autistic girls can be more likely to develop mental health problems such as anxiety, depression or obsessive compulsive disorder than boys (Hurley, 2014). They might also be at more risk of developing anorexia (Gould & Ashton-Smith, 2011; Solomon et al., 2012). This can mean their autism is perhaps not always spotted as difficulties are put down to the other identified condition. They might, therefore, spend longer without an autism diagnosis and not receive the type of support and understanding they need.
- Many autistic individuals with a more subtle presentation experience being dismissed by teachers, family or friends when they have suggested autism as a reason for their difficulties, or are originally given a wrong diagnosis by doctors (or told there was nothing wrong) as they don't fit the prevailing stereotype of an autistic person (Bargiela, 2019). This can again delay

diagnosis and cause further difficulties for the individual in question, resulting in them feeling they are not believed.

- Autistic females might be better at socialising and even give the appearance of being skilled in this area but it can often be a 'performance'. These skills may mean that females receive less tolerance and more expectation from others (Simone, 2010). As autistic females might have fewer 'obvious' autistic traits and might do a good job of 'masking' their autism, they might find, even with a diagnosis, that others don't 'see' the difficulties they are experiencing on a daily basis. This can mean they feel even more misunderstood.

The focus of this book is to explore how autism affects autistic girls who don't fit the stereotypical image of autism as this profile is still less understood and was, until recently, missed from the literature. The best way to understand life from autistic girls' perspectives is, of course, to hear from them themselves, and this is what you'll find in the next chapter.

Key points

- There have been different labels used to describe autism over the years. The term 'autism' or 'autism spectrum' includes those who would have previously been identified as having 'Asperger Syndrome'.
- All autistic individuals experience difficulties with social communication and interaction and with restricted, repetitive patterns of behaviour. They also experience sensory sensitivities, extreme anxiety, highly focused hobbies or interests, and meltdowns or shutdowns.
- Autism can be underdiagnosed in some cultures and communities.
- Studies suggest that between 1 in 100 and 1 in 44 people might be autistic. This is likely to be an underestimate.
- Females on the autism spectrum have until recently often been missed or misdiagnosed. They might not have such obvious difficulties as males, might be good at hiding, or masking, their difficulties, and might internalise difficulties, rather than express these openly. However, this more subtle presentation of autism can also affect males, and the more 'traditional' presentation can also affect females.

References

Attwood T. (2007) *The Complete Guide To Asperger's Syndrome*. London: Jessica Kingsley Publishers.

Bargiela S. (2019) *Camouflage: The Hidden Lives of Autistic Women*. London: Jessica Kingsley Publishers.

CDC (2021) *Community report on Autism 2021*, Autism and Developmental Disabilities Monitoring Network, Centre for Disease Control and Prevention, United States Department for Health and Human Services. Available from cdc.gov/ncbddd/autism/addm-community-report/documents/ADDM-Community-Autism-Report-12-2-021_Final-H.pdf [accessed 7 July 2022].

CIPD (Chartered Institute of Personnel and Development (2018) *Neurodiversity at Work*. London: CIPD.

Czech H. (2018) Hans Asperger, National Socialism and 'race hygiene' in Nazi-era Vienna. *Molecular Autism 9*, 29 (2018). https://doi.org/10.1186/s13229-018-0208-6

DSM-5-TR Diagnostic and Statistical Manual of Mental Disorders, *fifth edition, text revision*, American Psychiatric Association, 2022.

Gould J. & Ashton-Smith J. (2011) Missed diagnosis or misdiagnosis? Girls and Women on the autism spectrum. *Good Autism Practice Journal*, 12, 34–41.

Hallowell E.M., Ratey J.J. (2005) *Delivered from Distraction: Getting the Most Out of Life with Attention Deficit Disorder*. USA: Ballantine Books.

Hodkinson A. (2016) *Key Issues in Special Educational Needs and Inclusion*, second edition, London: Sage.

Hurley E. (2014) *Ultraviolet Voices: Stories of Women on the Autism Spectrum*. UK: Autism West Midlands.

Johnstone D. (2001) *An Introduction to Disability Studies*, second edition. London: David Fulton.

Lawson W. (2005) *Build Your Own Life*. London: Jessica Kingsley Publishers.

MQ Mental Health Research (2021) 'Mental health problems in autistic people'. Available from: www.mqmentalhealth.org/mentalhealth-and-autism/ [accessed: 15 November 2022].

NAS, National Autistic Society (2014) *Diverse Perspectives: The challenges for families affected by autism from Black, Asian and Minority Ethnic Communities*. National Autistic Society: London.

NAS, National Autistic Society (2022) *What is autism?* Available from autism.org.uk/advice-and-guidance/what-is-autism [accessed 7 July 2022].

Oxford Vaccine Group (2020) *MMR Vaccine: Measles, Mumps and Rubella*. Oxford University Vaccine Knowledge Report. Available from: vk.ovg.ox.ac.uk/vk/mmr-vaccine [accessed 07 July 2022].

PDA Society (2023) *About Autism and PDA*. Available from: pdasociety.org.uk/what-is-pda-menu/about-autism-and-pda/ [accessed 05 January 2023].

Simone R. (2010) *Aspergirls: Empowering Females with Asperger Syndrome*. London: Jessica Kingsley Publishers.

Skidmore D. (1996) Towards an integrated theoretical framework for research in special educational needs. *European Journal of Special Educational Needs Education 11*, 1, 33–42.

Solomon M., Miller M., Taylor S.L., Hinshaw S. & Carter C.S. (2012) Autism symptoms and internalising psychopathology in girls and boys with autism spectrum disorders. *Journal of Autism and Developmental Disorders*, 42, 48–59.

The Guardian (2022) Neurodiverse women sought for jobs at GCHQ and BAE Systems. *The Guardian Online.* Available from: theguardian.com/society/2022/nov/16/neurodiverse-women-sought-for-jobs-at-gchq-and-bae-systems [accessed on 16 November 2022].

Van Wijngaarden-Cremers P.J., Van Eeten E., Groen W.B., Van Deurzen P.A., Oosterling I.J. & Van Der Gaag R.J. (2014) Gender and age differences in the core triad of impairments in autism spectrum disorders: a systematic review and meta-analysis. *Journal of Autism and Developmental Disorders*, 44, 627–635.

Wing L. (1981) Language, social and cognitive impairments in autism and severe mental retardation. *Journal of Autism and Developmental Disorders*, 10, 31–44.

Part 3

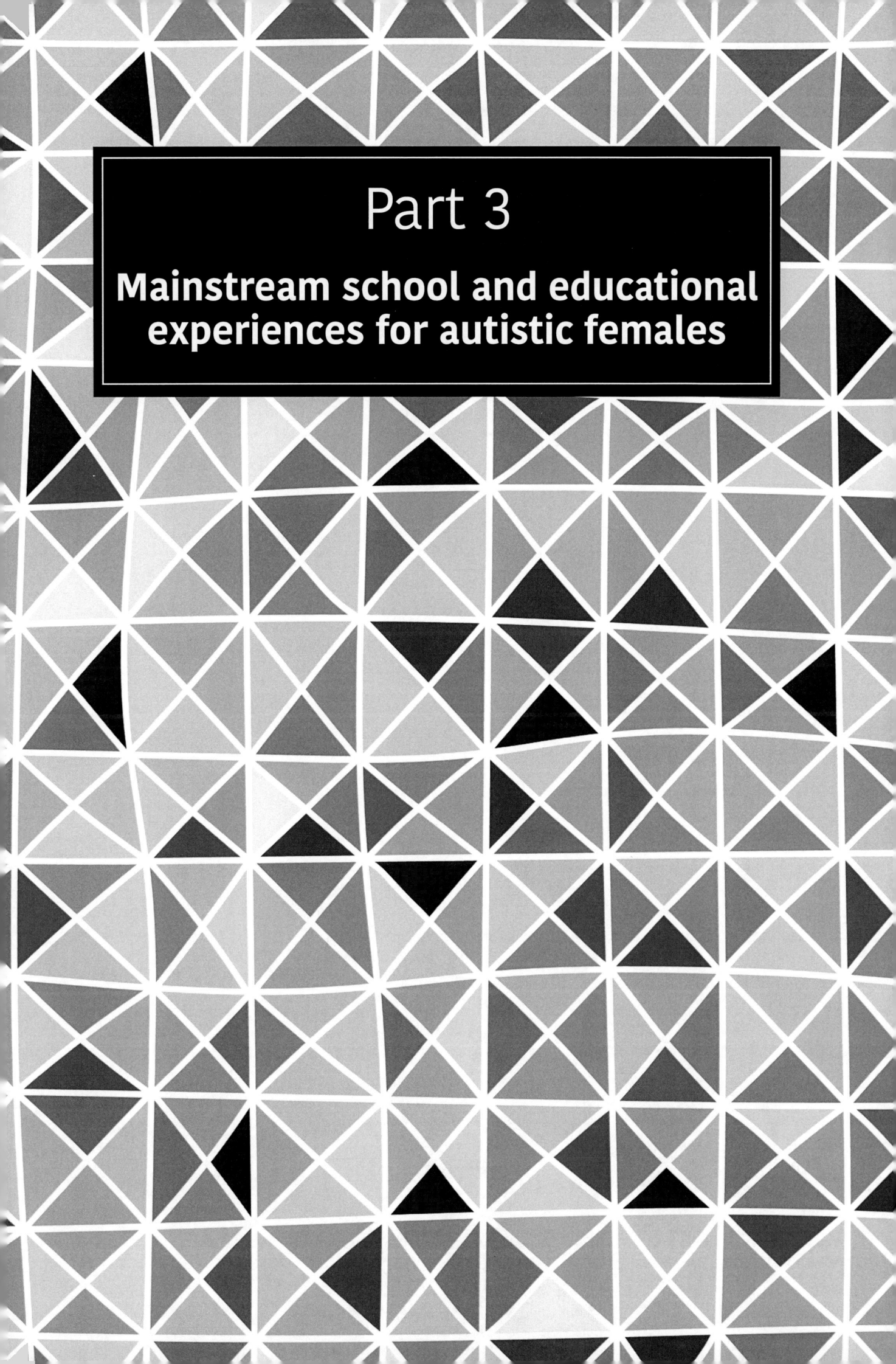

Mainstream school and educational experiences for autistic females

PART 3: MAINSTREAM SCHOOL AND EDUCATIONAL EXPERIENCES FOR AUTISTIC FEMALES

Introduction

I would like to thank the autistic girls and women who contributed to this section with anecdotes, insights and opinions from their educational experiences. The women who contributed all had a diagnosis of autism (including Asperger Syndrome) and were educated in mainstream environments. Some had received their diagnosis while they were at school and others were not diagnosed until later in life. From the experiences of the latter group we can learn a lot – how difficulties autistic individuals experience can be compounded by the added consequences of not receiving the right support or understanding.

The women diagnosed as adults have the benefit of hindsight and are able to reflect on their experiences, offering valuable advice about what would have been the most effective forms of support. The younger girls and women who contributed offer a different perspective: that of growing up with a diagnosis, and the positives and negatives that this brings.

It should be noted that not all the information in this section applies to every autistic student. The girls and women who contributed are reflecting on their personal, individual experiences. The suggestions and ideas provided are designed as guidance only and might not be what every individual student requires.

Insights from the women who took part have been grouped into the following topics for ease of reference:

- learning;
- communication;
- social media;
- social times;
- friendships;
- sensory issues;
- special interests;
- feelings and emotions;
- self-esteem;
- anxiety and absence from school;
- transition;
- puberty and growing up;
- interpreting the world.

As you'll soon learn, however, many of these issues cannot be considered in isolation – for example, sensory issues can affect how students are able to learn in class learning and their ability to communicate, which then impacts on self-esteem and increases anxiety. This increased anxiety can affect how able the student is to learn and concentrate and get on with others, plus might make them even more sensitive to sensory stimuli, and so the cycle goes on.

Note: The term 'autistic female' is used to cover autistic girls, young women, women and those who identify as women.

Learning

Learning – in the academic sense – is often seen as the main purpose of school – students go to gain the knowledge and qualifications needed for further education or employment. So, let's start by investigating how autistic girls get on with the learning aspect of school.

Subjects and activities

Let's start by taking a typical stereotype – that of the autistic maths genius or computer geek, happier with numbers or machines than with people. But how true is this? What are autistic girls' favourite activities? Do they even all enjoy the same things?

> At school I was passionate about languages and music so I was especially enthusiastic about being able to pursue these at high school in more depth. I especially loved taking part in concerts, and school exchange trips to Germany (Luna).

> I love creative arts such as drawing etc. (Autistic female 2)

> At school [primary] Lily-mai loves Art. She likes drawing, she finds it peaceful and fun. She prefers this to English and Maths. Lily-mai is really good at drawing and includes fine details to her drawings. She also enjoys spending time with her small group of friends. (Parent of Lily-mai)

> I was quite academic and enjoyed most subjects except practical ones. I was naturally talented at maths, I loved art and I loved the grammar aspects of Modern Foreign Languages, but not actually speaking in other languages. (Tori)

> I loved history and art. (Autistic female 10)

> Loved history and maths. (Autistic female 14)

> My favourite lessons are art and DT (Design and Technology). I like being able to do more practical and advanced stuff at high school. (Annie, Y7)

PART 3: MAINSTREAM SCHOOL AND EDUCATIONAL EXPERIENCES FOR AUTISTIC FEMALES

I'm naturally good at maths and find it easy. (Matilda)

I enjoyed English, writing stories and reading. I was very good with words; most of my intelligence is linguistic. I loved working on projects and making books about different topics. (Autistic female 15)

I was very good at reading and spelling and writing early. I loved playing music but once the teachers learnt I was playing by memory rather than reading music, I had to stop. I absolutely couldn't learn to read music no matter how hard I tried and so I had to hand my instrument back! I loved learning about the Vikings and runic language. (Autistic female 9)

I like art, textiles and English. (Autistic female 13)

I enjoyed French and science the most. (Autistic female 16)

My favourite lesson is animal care – I go to a farm once a week. (Loz)

I enjoyed science and found two teachers in particular were keen to support me. A good point was my music, taking part in operettas and being able to teach a younger student clarinet. (Autistic female 6)

I enjoyed art but often felt I wasn't very good at it. (Sue)

I had taught myself to read, write and do maths before I started school. I can't remember having to 'learn' these things. (Autistic female 12)

I enjoyed English literature. (Autistic female 20)

I found academic work easy and straightforward and gained a sense of achievement from getting high grades all the way through school. I excelled at seeing links between topics and concepts, and I could combine these in logical and watertight arguments which meant I did just as well at humanities as with maths and science. (Autistic female 17)

The one thing I did enjoy at school was art and graphics; it was nice to be expressive in a way that was not verbal or social. (Autistic female 18)

I was fairly academic and enjoyed learning. I used to come top [of the class] in examinations. (Autistic female 11)

Easily, my favourite thing [about school] was the lessons; I love learning, especially when it's something I'm passionate about! At school I could lose myself in art and writing. (Georgia)

Music is a big no-no – I can't tolerate the emotional music and loud noises (Autistic female 2)

I liked the structure. I loved Maths and Science as it was predictable and I was recognised for being smart. (Autistic female 1)

I liked learning new facts. I loved expanding knowledge and learning more about choices available for the future (Autistic female 8)

So, we can already see that autistic girls enjoy and do well at a variety of subjects; there is no particular subject area that suits them more than any other. But what about dislikes? Do all autistic girls find the same things difficult? Again, there is likely to be a range of responses, although lessons that require a large amount of socialising, sensory input or unpredictability are often mentioned.

I was terrible at coordination – I ran 'like a horse', and couldn't catch to save my life, apparently. It was an autism trait, but at the time, I just thought it was me. So, I had a note for nearly every PE lesson – I was ill, on my period, had forgotten my kit, had an appointment that lesson. I also avoided PE, because I was always chosen last for a team, and it hurt. (G)

I hated the smell of DT [Design Technology] rooms and the noise of the music room. I absolutely hated group work and less structured tasks. (Tori)

I didn't like registration or lunch or breaktime or any time where you had to be social, especially registrations which were always really long and dull. (Autistic female 4)

My least favourite subject was P.E. and I especially hated group sports and anything involving equipment such as hard balls as I was terrified of being hit! I also hated anything that involved having to perform in front of others! Of course, this meant that the other students would purposefully throw balls at me and teachers would pick on me to demonstrate things. (Luna)

I would like less writing tasks. I would prefer to be able to present work in other ways, for example, doing practical work and making something. (Annie, Y7)

Lily-mai dislikes maths, English and tasks like independent writing as she struggles with this. (Parent of Lily-mai)

PE was hideous as the whole experience was horrible – I hated gym kit; anything outdoors in the cold; swimming; having to get changed in front of others; getting yelled at by nasty, bullying PE teachers; being shamed for coming last or getting something wrong; being forced to work up a sweat and then given less than ten minutes to shower (in front of all the girls) and change before going into another lesson. Looking back, the unrealised sensory issues were a key part of this. (Autistic female 8)

PART 3: MAINSTREAM SCHOOL AND EDUCATIONAL EXPERIENCES FOR AUTISTIC FEMALES

I hated anything practical. I was clumsy and this was made worse due to anxiety of other people watching or having a time limit. I was always picked last for PE teams and just didn't know when it was my turn to get the ball, much to the frustration of my teammates. (LJ)

Proprioception

Proprioception (knowing where your body is in relation to other objects and people) can be a difficulty for some autistic students (see the later 'Sensory issues' section for further information. This can result in clumsiness, knocking things over, dropping things or misjudging personal space. It can have an impact in subjects such as PE, drama, dance, technology and other practical subjects, as well as socially.

Assemblies are just a waste of time. Tutor time is just pointless, we don't do anything. (Autistic female 5)

I was good at things like spelling, punctuation and grammar, but really struggled in English class – it was all about 'reading between the lines' and discussing characters' thoughts and emotions which I just couldn't do at all! Then having to write using 'wow words', which I just didn't get. As long as I got my message across, why did it matter that I'd said it in straightforward language rather than use flowery metaphors? I'd spend the whole lesson trying to think of a better word to use, so I wouldn't actually get anything written down at all. (Matilda)

Strengths and skills

Skills and strengths can be used across subject areas and learning experiences. Are there any skills and strengths that autistic women report being able to put to good use during their educational experiences? Structure, routine and consistency seem to suit many:

I liked the structure of the days, going from one lesson to the next. (Autistic female 4)

I enjoyed learning but preferred to work on my own. Most teachers forced me to work in pairs and groups with others who did not like me and bullied me. (Autistic female 6)

It's hard for me to identify many positives from my education, what I enjoyed most was spending daily structured time with my small group of close friends. I also liked having my time scheduled and knowing in advance what classes I would be in, however even that experience was tainted for me as I found the lessons themselves distressing. The positives didn't outweigh the negatives. (Alis)

> What I found most infuriating about university was the inconsistencies between the module study guide, handouts, and the tutor's own words. This increased my anxiety considerably. (Samantha)

> I liked the routines. I will never get the same routines in my life that I did in education. Being fed consistently at the same time and knowing what was coming next was something I didn't realise how much I'd miss. (May)

> I enjoy learning, stimulating my brain and the consistent routine. (Autistic female 3)

The ability to focus, concentrate, attend to detail and work hard on topics of interest is also something autistic females identify as a strength:

> I was able to focus for long periods, especially on reading (encyclopaedias and anything factual). (Autistic female 11)

> I had a good attention to detail. (Autistic female 10)

> I can work really hard. (Autistic female 13)

> I could focus on schoolwork for long periods of time and always got homework handed in on time as I didn't want to get into trouble. I did lots of extra reading and studying. I always followed the instructions and all of the rules so that I was never in trouble and got good marks. (Matilda)

> I had focus, determination and a real love of knowledge. I absorb new information quickly. (Autistic female 12)

> My strengths were perseverance and hyperfocus. I never gave up until I found a solution. I was also very imaginative – I spent a lot of time in my fantasy world but used this to write stories. (Autistic female 14)

> I worked quickly and always finished my work early. (Autistic female 10)

> If the teacher showed an interest in me and allowed me to show my strengths, then I would work even harder, even on areas that did not interest me as much. What I did enjoy, I would sail through much faster than the others. (Autistic female 15)

And other students report they are able to put organisation, the ability to follow instructions, perseverance, picking up new ideas and many other strengths to good use:

> I have a good imagination. (Loz)

> I studied psychiatric nursing for my degree and am now studying towards an Advanced Diploma in Canine Behaviour. Primarily being able to spend my time learning, rather than

working, was what was most beneficial about being in education. I spend my time naturally watching lectures, reading research papers and watching educational programs. Structuring my natural behaviours within a framework towards gaining qualifications is beneficial for me in guiding my learning effectively. I much prefer independent learning but also enjoyed lecture hall classes at university. I enjoyed producing good-quality work that got good marks. (Samantha)

I had good focus and concentration in class. I also worked really well independently and much preferred this to group work. I was well organised and always got all my homework in on time. I was good at following instructions and understanding what to do – I used to get so annoyed at classmates who didn't understand and made the teacher keep explaining things – I just wanted to get on with the work. My work was always neat and well-presented too. (Tori)

I don't give up when I don't understand. (LJ)

I'm not afraid to ask why, and I pick up on new, abstract concepts fast. At school I was like a little philosopher. (Autistic female 15)

I was a very logical thinker. (Autistic female 12)

I was very organised and well prepared. (Matilda)

I liked being helpful to teachers and being kept busy. (Autistic female 16)

My work was held up as an example of neat and precise presentation. (Autistic female 14)

I have a good imagination. I'm in my own story; it can be romance, horror or something like Alice in Wonderland. I daydream of adventures and wish I was a spy. (Loz)

I found it easy to learn facts and remember things. (Autistic female 11)

I liked getting plenty of feedback from tutors. (LJ)

I was good at listening and pointing out inconsistencies. (Autistic female 25)

I am able to focus on what interests me. I think outside the box and want to learn and understand. (Autistic female 19)

I can look at anything and make it identical; I have superb visual recall. (Autistic female 24)

I like making videos. (Autistic female 5)

I have a great sense of humour (Autistic female 13)

Any sort of research interested me. (LJ)

I enjoyed being challenged in class. (Autistic female 15)

I preferred to work independently and didn't need any help with the academic side of things. (Autistic female 11)

Not all autistic students are able to identify their skills and strengths; they might lack self-awareness, or even have been told that their strengths aren't strengths at all, but less 'desirable' characteristics:

I really have no idea whether I ever had any personal qualities that were considered strengths when at school, because I was consistently told that my personal qualities, such as being quiet, shy, and sensitive, were undesirable and I needed to overcome them if I wanted to achieve anything in life.

As a mature student at university, armed with the understanding of my neurodiversity and a better ability to advocate for myself, I was able to see that I actually have loads of strengths, including being very analytical and creative, and the ability to hyperfocus and do vast amounts of research. I gained very high grades for the majority of my assignments, possibly because I was good at considering all aspects of a topic or argument. I was consistently told that I write very well. (Luna)

Ideas for schools

Don't assume that all autistic students will like or dislike certain subjects. There are still often stereotypes of all autistic students being mathematical or computer geniuses – but in fact, autistic students have a wide range of talents and interests.

Support autistic students to identify and recognise their strengths and skills – some might not realise they have these strengths. Recognising strengths can lead to improved self-esteem and problem-solving skills.

Ensure students' strengths are recognised as strengths. Students who are always questioning and pointing out mistakes, for example, might be told that they are being irritating or inappropriate when, in fact, curiosity and good attention to detail can be a real strength (indeed, being able to identify inconsistencies quickly is a highly regarded skill in some careers, such as law and policing).

> Support students to apply their strengths to different parts of the curriculum and other aspects of life. For example, a student who is helpful or good at organising things, might be given responsibility for helping younger pupils, or organising the school library.
>
> *Please note: The ideas given in these boxes throughout this chapter will not all be suitable/ needed for every autistic student. They are designed to give a range of strategies for educators to choose from, try out and adapt according to their individual setting and students.*

Processing information

Success in education isn't just about learning facts or acquiring knowledge but more often about applying that knowledge to classroom tasks. This can be the downfall for many neurodivergent students – they often have more knowledge than most and a great understanding, but process information in a different way to their more neurotypical peers and find it hard to know how to apply this knowledge to classroom tasks in the way that is required.

> I was clever but didn't perform well in class. I later realised that this was because I needed more processing time before I made sense of things. I could never answer questions on the spot in class but understood things later when I went away to think about it and do homework. I would have been able to answer the questions well the next day once I'd had time to think about the topic, but by then it was too late, the teacher would be talking about the next thing. (Tori)

> More recently, as a mature student at university, I loved being able to research in depth on topics of interest. I was able to have quite a lot of say in the topics I studied (for example, I wrote my dissertations on autism and ADHD) and as a consequence was highly motivated! I was also able to do the majority of my studies online (mainly due to the pandemic!), which really suited me because I could work in my own way, at my own pace, and in my own environment. Having recorded lectures, for example, meant that I could listen as many times as I needed to, or access transcripts instead. I also enjoyed studying on my own and not having to fit in with other students! When I was at school (in the '80s and '90s) there was no knowledge of neurodiversity and I did not receive any help or support. I suppose that having a confident best friend was useful at times! As a mature student at university, I was given a huge amount of support including study skills tutors, a mentor, and various types of software (e.g. mind mapping) and equipment (e.g. an adjustable desk). I found transcripts to be invaluable because I take in information a lot quicker through reading. I also learnt to 'go with the flow' in how my brain works, rather than trying to fight against it. This meant working in different environments (e.g. different parts of the house, sitting on the floor or at the desk, outside) and different ways (e.g. on the computer or pen and paper, different colours and types of paper or pens). (Luna)

I find it difficult to understand how things are being taught and when teachers withhold necessary information. (Autistic female 2)

Auditory processing

Auditory processing (making sense of spoken information) can be a difficulty for many autistic individuals, even in autistic people who are highly articulate and intelligent. It is not a hearing problem, but a difficulty in extracting meaning from spoken language. Difficulties can be worse when there is a lot of background noise and when people are speaking quickly and giving lots of information.

It's helpful when tutors spend time explaining an assignment in a pragmatic way as normal descriptions provided often are far too vague and open to interpretation which I frequently misread. (Samantha)

I wish teachers would understand that I view the world in a different way and aren't just being difficult or awkward. Group tasks are incredibly hard, and I think teachers should be more understanding of how frustrating it can be when a group just doesn't work out. Maybe they should ask students to write someone they want to work with and someone they really don't? Also, being extra strict won't make the things we struggle with go away. It's not like it's our fault, as some teachers appear to think. (Autistic female 3)

Having a helper in lessons was a positive. (Autistic female 13)

I'm clever, but I can't learn like others. I like to take time to think things through. (Loz)

I need to process things in my own way. I need to go away and think about things and link them to my interests and what I already know. Then I am able to get my ideas and opinions, but by that time, everybody else has gone on to the next topic. (Matilda)

The struggles we may have with a particular subject can be the way it's taught to us. A different way of explaining, or a more in-depth tutorial if possible, may help enormously. My poor subject was maths. (Autistic female 16)

The all-singing, all-dancing lessons I had in school, and my daughter faces now, do not suit us all. Some of us have quieter ways of learning and need time. (Autistic female 22)

1:1 supervision, different teaching methods and quiet rooms are particularly helpful for me. (Autistic female 2)

PART 3: MAINSTREAM SCHOOL AND EDUCATIONAL EXPERIENCES FOR AUTISTIC FEMALES

Some autistic girls need to feel that the schoolwork had a 'point' to it for them to be able to engage fully. They have a strong need to understand the relevance of what they are learning. Others find it difficult to engage with topics that they are not interested in or that they have covered before.

> I found the work too easy and didn't see the point of wasting my time on it. If it had challenged me, I would have engaged more. (Autistic female 25)

> We can be incredibly bright and may seem 'disinterested' simply because normal teaching practices are going too slow for us. The lessons I achieved better in were those where the teacher recognised that I only needed 10 minutes of the hour lesson and was allowed to 'free learn' for the rest, even if it meant reading a novel. (Autistic female 23)

> Science always seemed pointless to me as I knew I didn't want to take it further. I've never needed to know about the periodic table or chemical formulas in real life, and I knew I wouldn't need them. There are lots of things that I have needed that we didn't learn in school. (Tori)

> Homework became a massive issue in secondary school; I resented having to give so much time to extra work outside the classroom and couldn't see the reason why. (Autistic female 8)

> I prefer to do my homework in school with help. (Autistic female 13)

> I don't like it when there's lots of noise and I also don't like having to do homework. (Annie, Y7) (Note from adult supporting Annie: Annie could do her homework at school, but she does not want to do this because it would mean having to miss out on breaktime or lunchtime.)

> I did like sociology and English literature very much, although if I did not like a text, I would refuse to study it much to the frustration of my teacher. I must have driven her crackers! (Autistic female 20)

Once again, it's clear that no 'one-size-fits-all' approach will work when it comes to autistic students. Some benefit from extra support in class, whereas others much prefer to teach themselves a topic. Some need more processing time to make sense of information, others learn new information quickly.

Ideas for schools

Autistic students might learn better if they are working in their own way. Get to know individual students and find ways of allowing them to use their preferred methods. Some, for example, learn more from teaching themselves.

Many autistic students benefit from increased time to process information. Try not to speak too quickly and pause after each piece of information to allow students time to absorb this. Build in longer wait times before expecting students to answer questions.

Use visual back-up for auditory information and instructions. Displaying instructions and information on the board can help some students who struggle to process auditory information. Refer to visuals when possible to support students' understanding (e.g. pictures, diagrams, flow charts, pictures, photographs, visual timetables).

Create 'pupil profiles' to share with staff in your setting (see Part 4 of this book for ideas). Make these in conjunction with your students. Students can include on their profile how they learn best, aspects of learning they find difficult and how they like to be supported.

Autistic students might also experience difficulties such as dyslexia, dyscalculia, dyspraxia, ADHD, learning difficulties or speech and language needs. Ensure that students get the support they require for any additional needs too.

Other autistic students might not have any apparent additional learning needs, so it can sometimes be difficult to understand why they are not reaching their potential. The difficulty might be with executive functioning skills, or due to anxiety or a need for perfection.

Executive functioning

Study skills, such as planning, preparing, organisation, time management, revision, research, essay writing and exam technique can also be a difficulty for some autistic students. These skills often require good executive functioning abilities and neurodivergent conditions such as autism and ADHD can have a huge impact on executive functioning.

Executive functioning

Executive functioning skills are those needed to plan and carry out tasks and organise our lives. These include skills such as planning, organisation, working memory, prioritising, task initiation, self-regulation and cognitive flexibility.

For every task we carry out, we subconsciously go through the following steps (taken from Bristol Autism Support, 2022). Most people go through these instinctively, but neurodivergent individuals might get stuck at one, or more, of these stages.

> **Organising:** What do I need to complete this task?
>
> **Prioritising:** What order do I do these steps in?
>
> **Remembering:** How did I do this last time?
>
> **Execution:** Let's do this thing.
>
> **Flexibility:** Do I need to do this differently?
>
> **Self-checking:** Did I do it right?
>
> In the classroom you might see students who do not know where to begin with a task, might miss out important steps within a task, who might seem to struggle with tasks they have done before or who might not be able to cope when something does not go exactly as planned.

When I left high school and started at sixth form college, I found that I lacked the skills to succeed with studying which, along with my lack of social skills, led to severe depression and eventually dropping out altogether. (Luna)

A big one with me would be that on those very rare occasions that I did ask for help, tutors dismissed me with an, 'Oh, don't worry; you'll be fine', as I was reasonably intelligent. However, this said nothing about my organisational skills, procrastinatory habits and difficulties understanding apparently aimless assignment briefs. (Autistic female 27)

It sounds easy saying, 'Do that essay by this date', but some of us need help making lists of what to do and then help doing it. (LJ)

It is very frustrating to be intelligent yet unable to study and succeed. (LJ)

When Annie (Y7) started being more independent and getting herself ready in the mornings, she was late for school a few times. Although the school generally has strict policies about punctuality, they make allowances on an individual basis and are supportive of Annie in becoming more independent. (Family member of Annie, Y7)

Many autistic girls are very capable, knowledgeable and intelligent, yet struggle to demonstrate this in class, as they learn or process information in different ways, or find executive functioning difficult. When considering things from a neurodiversity perspective, it's important to realise these ways aren't inferior to the more expected ways, simply different. Most school systems and teaching approaches are designed for only one way of learning and this can disadvantage students who learn differently.

What I am struggling with in my distance learning course is being marked by someone who I don't think knows much about dyslexia or even autism and ADHD. (Samantha)

I found having a mentor amazingly helpful and still do. (Autistic female 3)

Ideas for schools

Share the structure of the day. Use, and refer to during the day, a visual timetable (photos, symbols or words) so that students know what will be happening.

Share the structure of the lesson. Most students will benefit from knowing which tasks they'll be doing, in which order and how long they'll be spending on each one.

Break down tasks into manageable chunks. Provide visual prompts such as lists and step-by-step guides when possible. Visual instructions are more permanent and can be referred back to, supporting memory and the ability to work independently.

Remove distractions from the environment. A clutter-free classroom can support concentration and organisation.

Support students to find their own ways of organising themselves – for example, by setting alarms or reminders on their phone, using to-do lists or diaries, making voice memos. Support students to organise their work effectively – for example, by making folders for computer files or keeping equipment in a set place.

Use checklists to support students' ability to remember the correct equipment or tasks that need to be done.

Get to know individual students. Some might like a visual timer or countdown on screen so they know how long they have left of a task; others might find that the pressure of a 'ticking clock' increases anxiety and causes them to 'freeze'.

Homework may be problematic for some autistic students. Give students very clear instructions about what is expected, how much detail they need to give and which sources they are to use. Ensure that students are aware of extra support available such as homework clubs or mentors – although also consider that some students need their break/lunch/after school times to rest and re-set after being around people and learning all day. Consider whether the homework needs to be set in the first place – is it adding to learning?

Communication

Communication is a huge part of learning – and of every other aspect of school life. Language – whether spoken or written – is usually the medium through which students learn in the classroom – through listening, reading, writing, discussion or debate. Communicating with staff and other students is also important on a daily basis and difficulties with this can have an impact on both learning and wellbeing.

> ## Speech, language and communication
>
> ***Speech*** – The ability to articulate sounds in words. Speech also refers to fluency and clarity.
>
> ***Language*** – The rules which govern the way we assemble words to create sentences, conversations and longer narratives.
>
> ***Communication*** – Interaction between people, both verbal and non-verbal. This includes using language for different purposes, social skills, expressing emotions, facial expression, tone of voice and body language.

Differences in social communication and interaction are a core aspect of autism, as well as difficulties in using and understanding language. Let's investigate in more detail how this can feel for autistic women. For starters, even the thought of communicating can cause considerable anxiety for some:

Answering in class

> All through school I was just too terrified to talk to teachers. I'd get so anxious about it, I tried to avoid it at all costs and would try any other way to find out the information I needed. It was everything – having to put my hand up in class, finding a way to get heard or noticed, worrying I was asking a stupid question or wasting somebody's time, lacking in confidence to knock on a classroom door, not being able to articulate exactly what I meant. (Tori)

> Educational staff could help autistic students by not picking on them to answer a question if they don't want to. (Autistic female 4)

> I crumbled inside if a teacher asked me to read aloud in class. (Autistic female 10)

> It was difficult when teachers wanted everybody to speak out in lessons. (Autistic female 12)

> I hated talking in class. It was utterly embarrassing. (Matilda)

I often get into trouble for refusing to talk or not answering. (Autistic female 5)

I hated being asked questions as I was ridiculed for my very accurate and detailed answers. (Autistic female 6)

Teachers used to think I didn't know the answer. I did but just couldn't express myself quickly enough. I was only able to show my understanding when it came to written work which I had time to reflect on. I couldn't seem to put my sentences together in speech. (Autistic female 11)

I would advise schools to allow all pupils time to consider their responses; you get more frustration and 'rude' answers by constantly pressurising people to answer quickly (or they get told off for not listening/not doing the work!). Always preface questions/instructions with the person's name or with the words 'everyone' or 'class'. Don't always jump straight to telling pupils off for talking/chatting – consider if maybe the girl is asking for help from a classmate – it might be the first time she's ever worked up the courage to initiate conversation! (Autistic female 28)

Anxiety about speaking and answering in lessons might come about for a number of reasons for autistic students:

- Some worry about getting the answer wrong or being ridiculed by their classmates. Many autistic girls can experience low self-esteem or experience bullying, while others might have perfectionist traits or fear criticism.
- Some need more processing time than their peers to process and understand the question and then formulate their answer.
- Others may feel extremely uncomfortable if peers or staff are looking at them.
- Some might be concentrating so hard on following what is going on or on eliminating sensory distractions that they are unable to process sudden questions.

Experiencing anxiety like this often means the individual feels completely overwhelmed. Some teachers or parents report that autistic girls answer seemingly straightforward questions with a shake of the head, a 'No', or 'I don't know'. However, these 'I don't know' answers are often the truth – at that moment the student might be experiencing such anxiety, they are really unable to retrieve information that they clearly know. Unfortunately, in the classroom situation, this can sometimes be perceived as being deliberately difficult or not trying hard enough.

Non-verbal communication and paralanguage

Other difficulties with communication can arise due to sensory processing differences or differences with interpreting non-verbal communication cues. Some autistic girls, for example, can be very sensitive to sound. A normal loud 'teaching voice' may sound to them like the teacher is angry and always shouting. Some autistic students can find it particularly difficult to look at somebody when listening as there is just so much visual and aural information to process at the same time (Winter & Lawrence, 2011). Others might not understand, not use or might 'see through' social niceties and social conventions, which may appear pointless or even 'fake'. Some might not show the 'expected' facial expression, others might have difficulty with understanding and using the expected tone of voice or intonation.

> When you think I'm not listening because I'm not looking at you, I actually am. I don't like looking into people's eyes; it makes me feel uncomfortable. (Autistic female 5)

> Teachers often thought I wasn't interested because of my lack of facial expression or they thought I wasn't bothered by things that were causing me huge amounts of anxiety on the inside, just because I wasn't expressing this on the outside. (Matilda)

> People say I always laugh at the wrong time or at the wrong thing. (Autistic female 13)

> I wish her teachers and peers knew that if her face looks unhappy it doesn't mean she isn't happy and that she doesn't have the weight of the world on her shoulders. (Parent of Lily-mai)

> I didn't know that eye contact was important until somebody explained it to me. (Loz)

> I didn't like teachers who were always shouting or who had loud voices. Also teachers who didn't give me time to think or who misunderstood my answers. Also, I can tell if people aren't really interested so didn't like teachers who gave false praise or who were being fake or just pretending to be a nice person. When I didn't look like I was listening, I was actually concentrating really hard. If I'm trying too hard to show that I'm listening by doing all the facial expressions and nodding and eye contact, then actually my attention is on this, not on what the other person is saying. (Tori)

Autistic individuals are often judged by neurotypical expectations – so it is assumed that the student not making eye contact or an expected facial expression is uninterested. The student in question might actually be very interested and be trying harder than most to concentrate.

Social communication and expectations

The complex social relationships and expectations relating to figures in authority can be a mystery to some autistic girls and they might not pick up on these innately. Others may know what is expected socially, but it still might make no real sense to them. Often, autistic individuals can be very honest, might not understand why people lie and might say exactly what they think (Winter & Lawrence, 2011). This bluntness can have some negative consequences in the classroom which, in most school systems, is based on the idea of an authority figure who should not be questioned. In other situations, these traits can be a positive, especially when used to bring about change or challenge the status quo. As autistic climate activist Greta Thunberg (2019), when asked by TV reported what gave her the confidence to speak truth to power, explained 'I am on the autism spectrum so I don't really care about social codes in that way'.

> I was always questioning, especially if something didn't make sense. I used to correct the teachers a lot when they made a mistake, but I don't think many would see that as a positive point! (Autistic female 25)

> I always got on better with adults than my peers, who I thought were mostly very immature. I approached teachers as if I were an adult too, on their wavelength, and I think some thought I was being rude or not respecting their authority. (Autistic female 12)

Many autistic girls try hard to communicate 'in the right way' with others but find they somehow seem to say the wrong thing.

Autistic comedy writer, Sara Gibbs, explains how differences in communication style can even lead to autistic individuals being seen as untrustworthy: 'You try to explain yourself, your body language and facial expressions don't match your words, adding to the perception that you're not to be trusted. When you finally meltdown because you are overwhelmed by your environment or frustrated at not being heard, you're berated for being dramatic.'

Some autistic girls noted that their relationships with teachers seemed to be different to other students'. Some felt invisible, overlooked or misunderstood, perhaps as a consequence of their differences in their verbal and non-verbal communication styles. Some autistic girls noted that a teacher who 'got' them could make all the difference, inspiring and motivating them to work hard.

> I liked teachers who were honest and showed an interest in me. (Autistic female 10)

> I worked hard for the teachers I liked but not for those who didn't inspire me. (Autistic female 16)

> When my art teacher left, we got a new teacher who I felt just took a dislike to me (this happened a lot and I never knew why), and I would skip class. (Autistic female 26)

> The main negative for me during my school years was being completely overlooked. I was quiet, and I didn't create any trouble, so I did not receive any attention, and I did not feel or know how to ask for any. The teachers were always busy dealing with the students who made the most noise, and when the other children became noisy and troublesome, I would sit quietly. I hated the shouting. I was not placed in a high class form, so the teacher never expected much from me; I didn't realise this, and I had high expectations of myself. I remember doing some homework; I had to design a poster. I decided to create a new font design for the poster and each letter was meticulously done. When I brought it in, the teacher did not believe I had done it because it was believed to have been too good to be my own. They thought my

parents had done it. The teachers did not know me or know my potential because most of the time I was invisible to them. (Autistic female 29)

As I wasn't diagnosed with autism until I'd left school at 18, I was never accommodated properly. The few strategies in place were not consistent and completed begrudgingly by many staff who were under the impression I was attention seeking. The strategies put in place by my high school were things like not being called to talk in class, extra time in assessments/homework due to my processing speed, the ability to choose a preferred seat in class and print outs of information rather than given verbally. Had these strategies been completed consistently I believe I would have benefitted however certain teachers ignored them, lost interest in helping after time went by or altered them to fit what they found easier to fulfil. Strategies I wish had been in place include a quiet room to go to if I was overstimulated or anxious (after all eating lunch in the school bathrooms isn't very hygienic) and a mentor or teacher who actually cared about my wellbeing to advocate on my behalf. (Alis)

Honesty is a trait often associated with autism; many autistic people say they are told they are too honest and that their honesty causes offence where none was meant. Autistic people can tend to state the facts or reality of a situation, whereas neurotypicals can focus more on what is most socially acceptable or expected.

Sara Gibbs, in her 2021 autobiography, Drama Queen, explains the consequences of this: 'One thing I've learned the hard way from a lifetime of non-optional honesty is the more boldly you speak the truth, the quicker people will be to accuse you of being a liar.'

Theory of mind

Theory of mind – or the double empathy problem

'Theory of mind' means the ability to understand the thoughts, feelings and actions of other people. It is the ability to see things from another's perspective, to put ourselves in somebody else's shoes. It has often been considered one of the things that autistic people find difficult.

However, the 'double empathy problem' (a term coined by autistic researcher Damian Milton) suggests that this is not a one-sided difficulty but that neurotypical individuals have as much difficulty understanding autistic people, as autistic people have understanding neurotypicals. The difficulty is on both sides. After all, if neurotypical people understand autistic people well, there would not need to be all the books, training courses, awareness campaigns and autism charities trying to improve understanding.

For some autistic girls difficulties with theory of mind make communication with teachers difficult or just downright confusing.

> I hated teachers asking me questions. If I didn't know the answer, I would think that they must have known I didn't know and had deliberately asked me to make me look stupid in front of everybody in the class. If I did know the answer, I would wonder why they had asked me such a simple question. The answer seemed so obvious and surely everybody knew it, so why were they asking? Was it to trick me? Was it to make me look a show-off in front of my classmates? (Tori)

Differences for autistic girls with theory of mind and empathy are discussed in more detail later in the 'Feelings and emotions' section.

Some autistic students might give much more information than is expected when they answer a question, especially if it is related to a topic of interest to them. 'Infodumping' is a term used to describe this habit of giving a lot of extremely detailed information in a single go. Autistic writer, Laura James, describes in her 2017 autobiography 'Odd Girl Out' (p. 18), 'This is a classic autistic info dump. I have all these thoughts in my head and I have to get them out. Even if the listener is so bored they are contemplating throwing themselves off a cliff to get away from my incessant chatter, I simply cannot stop.'

Ideas for schools

Some autistic students may have difficulties communicating through spoken language. Allow students to use different ways to communicate (e.g. through email, writing or drawing) so that they can communicate with staff.

Create opportunities to get to know pupils individually. Some autistic students might feel more comfortable if they have had the opportunity to get to know the teacher first.

Speaking in class can cause considerable anxiety for some autistic students. Try allowing more time before expecting answers. You could also build in time for students to prepare their answers, or give them the opportunity to rehearse with a classmate first. Some might benefit from being allowed to refer to notes or visuals.

Some autistic students' sensory sensitivities can impact on communication. A loud 'teaching voice', for example, might be interpreted as shouting or as the teacher shouting, being angry or in a bad mood.

Be honest. Admit when you have changed your mind or when you do not know something. This can reduce anxiety for some autistic students.

> Be aware of your individual triggers. If you find yourself easily irritated with a student who questions you, contradicts you or does not seem to respect your authority, ask yourself why. Now try and see the world from the student's perspective. Most autistic students are not deliberately being disrespectful, simply honest.

Group work

Communicating with peers can be difficult for autistic students. Many autistic individuals report relationships with peers as having had a hugely negative impact on their learning as well as on their self-esteem and wellbeing. Group work is a particular difficulty for many:

> I enjoyed very structured lessons without group or pair work. I liked teachers who kept control of the class. I understood what was happening in lessons and picked up new things quickly. However, I couldn't keep up in class discussions or group work because of the dynamics of group conversation – I was never able to contribute. For this reason people thought I couldn't understand. (Tori)

> I like to work with other quiet people. (Loz)

> Group work was horrendous. I got very frustrated with the other pupils and felt they didn't listen to me. I hated being put in a group with pupils who would mess about or didn't understand the work. I felt they were bullying me as they wouldn't let me get on with the work, and then I felt that the teacher was bullying me too, by forcing me to work with these pupils! (Autistic female 11)

> I wish teachers wouldn't make me work with people who don't like me. (Autistic female 5)

> Nobody wanted to work with me because I wasn't popular and didn't say much. I didn't know how to contribute to group conversation. (Matilda)

> I don't like team games. (Autistic female 13)

> I hated group work because I had no friends. If the children arranged themselves into groups, I would have nobody to go with, and if the teacher arranged the groups, the other pupils would make it clear I was an undesirable. (Autistic female 12)

> Anxiety over group work plagued me so much that in the end, I wasn't capable of it – I grew tired of being told by my peers: 'No, you can't work with us. The group is too full – maybe next time?' Next time never came, I wanted to yell! Due to this, I never got in a group when the teacher told us to; it was up to them to physically put me in a group, which only made me look worse. (G)

Understanding others' intentions is also a difficulty for autistic students:

> In my first week at secondary school, two girls in my English class asked if they could borrow some of my coloured pencils. I said yes, as I was always a kind and helpful child. Within minutes they were sharing my pencils with their friends, throwing them around to each other. Some rolled on to the floor; one broke as somebody tried to sharpen it; one boy was chewing on the end of one. I started to panic and become really anxious. Would I get them all back? What if I lost some? How would I be able to do my art homework that evening? Would I really have to touch a pencil that had been in somebody else's mouth? I didn't want that one back. It was just too disgusting! I felt physically as if I was going to vomit. I couldn't concentrate on my work as I was so worried about my pencils and was trying to pick them from the floor. I was just upset and horrified. I never would have been so inconsiderate with somebody else's property. I was almost in tears by the end of the lesson but didn't want to say anything because I thought people would say I was being silly. The next time I didn't want to share my things because I knew people weren't considerate and would lose or break them, but then I got told that I was the one being selfish. It always seemed to be like this – I was the one being inconsiderate; other people were just being 'normal'. (Tori)

> The social dynamic of school was always an issue. In primary school I had it easy, we were young enough that the things that made me different made me interesting and being blunt was normal communication. However, during high school that all changed as, especially with girls, communication because more confusing and passive aggressive. People started to not mean what they said and there was this unspoken conversation people seemed to have that I was left out of. (May)

> Education staff need to improve their awareness and the supports that are in place to help autistic students. Communications with autistic students being consistent and clear in all formats would help, especially in written course-related documents. Also, managing class dynamics well… Not allowing the dominant students to dominate all aspects of class. (Samantha)

Ideas for schools

Don't assume autistic girls will learn group working skills simply by being made to work with others. Being forced to work with other students who they do not feel comfortable with may cause extreme anxiety which can outweigh any benefits that might be gained through the task. Consider whether the task really needs to be completed as a group.

> Some autistic students might need to develop group-working skills slowly. They could start with a short task with a supportive peer, or complete work individually which is then shared in a small group or put together with other students' work to create a larger piece.
>
> Allocate groups. Saying, 'Get yourselves into groups' or 'Pick your own teams' can increase some students' feelings of being left out or unpopular if nobody volunteers to work with them.
>
> Teach all students regularly what is meant by effective group-working skills. Ensuring that all students are clear about the expectations will help all group members stay on task and work together effectively. This will then have a positive impact on any autistic students too. Autistic girls can often be very good at learning and remembering rules. They might know exactly what is meant by working in a group but be confused because it is the other pupils who do not appear to be following these rules (e.g. by talking 'off task', by interrupting, not sharing the work equally, etc.). This is the confusing element. They have learned the rules, but others do not necessarily follow these!
>
> Try allocating specific roles within the group (e.g. note taker, timekeeper, questioner). This can support all students to play an active role.

Using and understanding language

Difficulties in using and understanding language can also cause difficulties for autistic students. We've already learned about potential difficulties with auditory processing. Some have a literal understanding of language. Some might struggle to 'read between the lines' or make inferences which appear to be obvious to their peers. Others might not realise when people are exaggerating, being sarcastic or just using common social conventions. These things can lead to misunderstandings and disappointments.

> I struggle to understand the questions in class. (Autistic female 13)

> I found English comprehension difficult because many of the exercises required reading between the lines which I could not do but learned to get better at as I got older. (Autistic female 10)

> I had no problems writing factual essays for most subjects but hated writing for English lessons where the emphasis was on using fancy words, complex sentences and interesting expressions. I didn't have such a wide vocabulary as my peers. (Tori)

> In primary school we once had to paint a picture of a ship in a storm. The teacher told me I should make my ship a bit darker. I went over it in black paint. The teacher then asked me

why I had ruined my picture! I still remember the confusion to this day. Why don't people say exactly what they mean? I thought I'd been following her instructions. (Matilda)

Other difficulties using and understanding language for autistic students can include:

- Echolalia – repeating words or phrases that others use
- Using language very precisely
- Sounding more 'formal' than others
- Difficulties picking up on implied meaning ('It's getting noisy in here' – actual meaning 'You need to be quieter')
- Giving literal answers ('Can you tell me what year WWII began?' 'Yes.')

Ideas for schools

Convey instructions and information in straightforward language to avoid confusion and misunderstandings. Use as few words as necessary.

Say exactly what you want to happen; not all autistic students will pick up on implied meaning (e.g. 'It is getting very noisy in here'; not all will realise this means you want them to stop talking as you've made a comment rather than given an explicit instruction).

Check understanding by asking students to show you what they have to do or to explain in their own words. Some might repeat back the instructions given without actually understanding what they have to do.

Ensure questions and instructions are clear and unambiguous (e.g. 'Circle the biggest number' – do you mean the largest amount, or the largest font size?).

Be aware that some autistic students may struggle to understand idioms, metaphors and figurative language such as common sayings and expressions. Explain these when you use them.

Try giving sentence starters to support students to formulate their answers and responses.

Social media

For many young people, including autistic girls, social media is an important part of their lives – a way to keep in touch with friends, to keep up-to-date with what's going on, to follow celebrities they admire, and to connect with others with similar interests.

Some studies show that autistic people prefer to communicate via social media (Begley, 2014; Kranjc, 2011) as they find it provokes less anxiety than communicating face-to-face or via telephone. Some autistic people find that not having to worry about facial expressions, eye contact and tone of voice helps them to be able to communicate. Other advantages of online communication can be having more time to consider a reply and to process the information given by others.

Some autistic people also find that social media is the only place they have been able to meet people with similar difficulties and differences and value their online friendships and support circles; they might find sanctuary online in a place that appears to feel safer and more comfortable than 'real life' (Shane-Simpson et al., 2016). There are also young people active on YouTube and other social media platforms who are working to increase awareness of neurodiversity. For young people, this can be the easiest way of gaining information about their neurodivergency, as well as giving them role models who help them see their neurodivergence as a positive, different way of being.

Of course, social media also has its downsides. The negative aspects of social media for the general population are often discussed. Parents' and teachers' concerns usually include cyberbullying, sexting, connecting with strangers, harmful or inappropriate content, scams, and the effect on young peoples' sleep and wellbeing. There can be additional concerns for autistic girls – worries that they might be especially vulnerable online due to their communication difficulties, difficulties with social understanding, low self-esteem and possible real-life social isolation. Online communication might not necessarily be easier for autistic individuals either – sarcasm and humour might be harder to interpret without additional contextual clues, and comments can easily be misinterpreted. It can also be easy to type, or agree with, comments that can be misinterpreted with others – meaning that autistic individuals might not only be more vulnerable to online bullying, but might also, inadvertently, contribute to bullying. Some research studies (Finckenauer et al., 2012) also suggest that autistic individuals can be at higher risk of addiction and compulsive use of social media.

Let's hear about some social media experiences:

> I'm so glad that social media wasn't such a big thing when I was at school. I find it hard enough to navigate as an adult. I can't imagine having to deal with all of that at school. I see things that others have written on social media and find myself getting really angry – even

when the posts have nothing to do with me at all. I don't know whether it has something to do with absorbing others' emotions or just getting frustrated that people don't understand things and don't do the most basic research before they post. (Matilda)

I love watching YouTube videos and making my own. Mostly people make nice comments. (Autistic female 5)

I get depressed when I see photos on Facebook of friends or colleagues who have been out and not invited me. It feels like they're not only excluding me but then boasting about it by posting the photos. (Autistic female 12)

I have a love–hate relationship with social media. I'd rather not be on it, but find it's the only way some people will keep in touch and the only way to find out what's going on locally. I've learned a lot about my autism from social media too. It's the only thing that's accessible to many people. But the algorithms really don't help the way my brain works. They feed in to my overthinking and anxiety. (Tori)

Ideas for schools

Teach online safety and be aware that autistic girls might be especially vulnerable online. They might need extra guidance on understanding others' intentions. They might also not be ready for this teaching at the same time as their peers. Some autistic students might also need different ways of this online safety being taught – for example, some prefer written information which they can read through at their own pace and keep to refer back to, rather than having to rely on remembering what was said in class.

Liaise with parents and carers about online safety and suggest ways they can best support their children and young people online.

Have clear policies in school about what constitutes cyberbullying, how students are to report this, and what the outcomes will be. Ensure all students know it will be taken as seriously as real-life bullying.

Social media sites can be blocked from being accessible on school equipment, and students can be banned or discouraged from bringing their own mobile devices onto the school premises to reduce the amount of cyberbullying or other difficulties during school hours. Some schools have policies where mobile devices must be handed in at the beginning of the day and collected at the end. Consider what could work best for your setting.

PART 3: MAINSTREAM SCHOOL AND EDUCATIONAL EXPERIENCES FOR AUTISTIC FEMALES

> Work on students' self-esteem. Some students might feel they have to be on social media platforms but in fact, would prefer not to be. Help all students to see that it is okay to make that choice if that is best for them at the time. Some students might need support to understand social media companies' algorithms and how they can block or reduce certain content appearing in their feeds if this would be beneficial to them.

Social times

School isn't only about learning. Some people make friendships at school or university that last their entire lives and others enjoy the social times during the school day that offer an opportunity to chat and play with others. However, for many autistic girls, these unstructured times during the school day often pose the most difficulties. Communication in the classroom often has a specific purpose and the focus is on completing the work set. Social times, however, lack the same structure, routine and clear rules. At secondary school especially, students are often left to organising themselves without adult guidance. Social times can sometimes be when autistic girls feel most lonely, isolated and different. Autistic comedian Hannah Gadsby (2022) explains how her preference for solitude was seen as something out of the ordinary: 'I was at my happiest in my own company, which I took to be an abnormality. It never occurred to me that it could be the epitome of normal behaviour – for me.'

> The social aspect was difficult particularly when I was in a class that was not the top class. The top class was a safe haven for me. I needed structure in the classroom and minimised down time which equalled social interaction. There was not many clubs etc. and I didn't know I was Autistic or that I had ADHD. I found joining in with sports at lunch provided more structure but only when it was organised by a teacher. (Autistic female 1)

> Playtime was often very difficult: I was terrified of being hit by balls from the various games played by the boys and wasn't comfortable with the 'girl' options – playing on the monkey bars/swings or sitting chatting/making daisy chains. (Autistic female 8)

> I found being in the library during lunchtime and breaktimes helpful. (Autistic female 4)

> I hated break and lunchtimes as I had nothing to do and no friends to be with. I used to dread these times. I couldn't sit on my own in the canteen and didn't particularly want to join in with the others; their games and chat didn't seem fun. I hid a lot in the toilets. I felt as if everybody was looking at me being by myself and was totally embarrassed. At sixth form college it was different; I made some friends, and it was OK to sit by yourself with a hot chocolate and some studying in the dining area or go to the library. (Tori)

> Break times were awful until I made some real friends when I was 14. (Autistic female 12)

> Social elements were definitely the hardest. Being bullied at primary school was tough, and I didn't tell my parents about most of it until years later. Also hated PE, and the noisy lunch room. A teacher used to let me stay in her classroom at break, but then she had to stop as apparently it wasn't fair on the other kids. (Sue)

Some autistic girls might want to spend 'social' times alone but feel that this is seen as unusual or unacceptable. Many autistic individuals find being around other people exhausting. Simply interacting with others in lessons can take up a lot of energy, and they might need time away from people to recover from this. Others might want to join in with peers but not know how to, or feel they keep 'getting it wrong', intensifying feelings of being different and low self-esteem. Difficulties for some might not at first be obvious to observers. Some autistic girls develop the ability to 'disappear' in a large group and, although physically present, do not actively participate, being on the 'periphery of social interaction' (Holliday Willey, 1999).

> I would beg the teacher to let me stay in at playtime and organise the library, and when he made me go out, I played on my own, digging in the dirt. In secondary school I often used to eat my lunch in the toilets or go to the library and read psychology books to figure out what the hell was wrong with either (a) me or (b) everybody else! (Autistic female 19)

> Let girls be on their own if they want to. (Autistic female 13)

> It would help to have a quiet place to think and meditate, without the world disturbing you. (Loz)

> Don't insist that we participate in everything other people do. Don't make us feel odd if we don't have friends; treat our preferences as normal. (Autistic female 11)

> When I was 11, I began to spend break and lunchtimes reading to the infants. I enjoyed this far more than having to navigate the friendships of my peer group. I felt that I was on a different wavelength and didn't find their conversation interesting. Suddenly it seemed my classmates had gone from being normal girls to being gossipy, secretive and just totally incomprehensible creatures who would fall out, make up and totally contradict themselves. (Matilda)

> Let girls sit on their own if they want to. School is for learning, and there is too much pressure to be sociable all of the time. (Autistic female 13)

In the school playground, there is often a set of 'unwritten rules' which can be incomprehensible or unknown to autistic students. These can range from the more obvious (you do not tell the teacher if classmates have done something slightly against the rules) to the more complex nuances of female social communication, which can also differ from group to group. As autistic writer, Laura James (2017, p. 58), explains, 'The girls at school seemed to have had a secret briefing that informed them of exactly how to behave. When they huddled together in the playground, conversations bounced without missing a beat from boys to cherry-mint lip-gloss'. Also, some autistic girls might play differently than their more typically developing peers. They may prefer games that mimic reality or that they can be in control of. Their play may also remain imaginative or 'childish' into adolescence, which can make them vulnerable as they become older (Winter & Lawrence, 2011). Some autistic girls found that they enjoyed social times if they were engaged with activities they enjoyed.

> I enjoyed helping in the library and was very good at keeping the books tidy and in the right place. (Autistic female 10)

> I found safety in attending lunchtime and after-school groups such as orchestra and choir. I also volunteered in the school library or went home for lunch so I could avoid bullies. (Autistic female 6)

> I like being with my best friend and having somewhere safe to go back to. (Loz)

> I loved helping out in the library. Having a best friend who was on the spectrum helped a lot too. (Autistic female 21)

> I was kind to the younger girls and helped them with reading at break and lunchtimes. (Matilda)

> I like to play games on my phone at lunch time. It helps me feel less stressed. (Autistic female 13)

> I liked having quiet time by myself and being able to read. (Autistic female 12)

Ideas for schools

Social times can be a source of great anxiety for some autistic girls. Some may be exhausted from the social contact of the classroom and may benefit from having a quiet place to go to relax, read or draw. They might just need this 'alone time'.

Autistic students can have difficulties engaging with their peers and may not enjoy socialising in the more typical ways. Offering a range of activities during social times can be helpful, including some that do not require too much interaction, such as homework clubs, computer clubs or art clubs.

Social times can be opportunities to pursue interests and meet like-minded people. Some autistic girls can find it easier to communicate with others when taking part in a structured

> activity or if they find they have a shared interest. Encourage students to find extracurricular clubs that they might be interested in (films, chess, board games, arts and crafts, reading).
>
> Many autistic students dislike being made to feel different at school. They might recognise that they need something different but do not want to be seen as different or 'odd'. Support this by ensuring all needs are seen as equally valid and 'normal', offering all options to all students. Ensure that preferences to spend time alone, for example, are not seen as 'inferior' to other preferences, but instead make all students aware that quiet areas are available to anybody who wants to use them. This helps to remove any stigma attached to doing something different.

Friendships

For many young people, friendships are what makes school enjoyable; autistic females, however, often cite connecting with others as one of their main difficulties. Autistic author, Elle McNicholl (2023) explains how she wanted friends but found others found her differences off-putting: 'I wanted to be everyone's friend, but no one wanted to be mine. I was told I was weird and strange and that there was "something wrong with me".' Autistic girls might have slightly different friendships than others, perhaps preferring to socialise with older or younger students, or wanting only one friend, rather than a group of friends. Some prefer their own company. Others prefer the company of adults or may have a concept of friendship which is a few years behind that of their peers (Attwood, 2007).

> I made some lifelong friends once we were placed into our GCSE classes. (Autistic female 10)

> I always found the social aspect of school difficult. Other children always made me very stressed and I often accidently said something that would offend or upset them and couldn't understand why they felt like that. (Autistic female 3)

> I had very few friends, was bullied and hated being forced to work with a partner or small group who would bully or exclude me. The school playground was an area of dread. (Autistic female 12)

> My most obvious difficulties were social – I had very few friends and was bullied horribly all the way through school. I found the social and sensory demands of the canteen horrifying and stopped going there when I was 14 because it was easier to skip lunch than endure having nobody to sit with and the loud, smelly, bright environment which led to me developing an eating disorder. (Autistic female 30)

> The negatives were having very few friends, bullying, being forced to work with a partner or small groups with others who bullied me or excluded me. The school playground was an area

of dread. Teachers would also make fun of me which became as upsetting as the bullying. (Autistic female 31)

The headteacher was genuinely shocked when he realised the amount of bullying I had kept hidden. The fear of consequences of telling anyone left me suffering alone. (Autistic female 6)

Once I got to the last two years of school, we were put into GCSE classes, and I met some lovely, quirky girls who I am still friends with today – a saving grace! (Autistic female 9)

I had some friends in Year 7 who I'd been in primary school with, but they distanced themselves from me when I started to get bullied. (Autistic female 11)

A difference between primary and secondary school is also often noted by autistic girls and their families. Primary school playtimes are often more structured ('wet play' activities or semi-structured games in the playground such as hopscotch, skipping or climbing frames), whereas the emphasis during social times at secondary school is often on chatting in friendship groups.

Girls' friendships also tend to become more complicated in secondary school, which can cause additional difficulties for autistic girls. During adolescence, the nature of friendships changes for all young people, with more of an emphasis on peer group acceptance. Girls' friendships with one another are usually more intimate than those between boys, with girls reporting high levels of caring, sharing, trust and loyalty, whereas boys spend more time on shared activities and less time sharing secrets and discussing feelings (McGhee et al., 2011). This shift from childhood friendships to friendships that are deeper, more emotional and personal can be particularly difficult for autistic girls who can find it difficult to connect on a social and emotional level with peers and who may find it easier to interact when taking part in special interests or structured activities (Simone, 2010).

I'm not interested in what the other girls talk about – it all seems a waste of time. (Loz)

I didn't have many friends outside of school but got on OK with my classmates. It was only during my final two years at primary school that I really started to realise I was different from the other girls. Their chatter and gossip seemed pointless, and I preferred to sit by myself or read to the younger pupils. I hated it when other pupils were emotional, upset or cried as I couldn't understand why; it seemed a pointless interruption to the learning. (Matilda)

Although being part of a larger friendship group is often difficult for autistic girls, relating on a one-to-one level can be somewhat easier. Autistic girls might have one special friend and can worry about what their peers think about this (Gould & Ashton-Smith, 2011). A friendship such as this can be intense (to both sides) and can also cause much anxiety or upset when things change.

I had a best friend all through primary school but couldn't cope when we went to secondary school and she wanted to be friends with other people too. (Matilda)

For some autistic females there can be difficulties in understanding others' feelings and perspectives. An example of this is assuming that others no longer want to be friends, perhaps because of a perceived mistake they've made, or because the other person has a new friend. Sara Gibbs, in her autobiography 'Drama Queen' (2021, p. 76) describes how she was often the one to end friendships, relationships or workplace friendships due to her embarrassment or shame about having done the wrong thing: 'Sometimes people would stop calling, or dump me or fire me. But most commonly I would pre-empt them by disappearing or burning bridges out of shame. I would run the moment I had been "found out".'

Ideas for schools

Provide a range of activities on offer during social times for girls to engage with; usual expectations of socialising on the playground with friends might be a source of great frustration.

Some students may benefit from working with an adult to unpick a situation. As one autistic 15-year-old I met explained, 'I want somebody to help me to understand how friendships work and why things have happened.'

Some autistic girls might find it easier to get on with students who are older or younger than themselves rather than their immediate peer group. Create opportunities for this.

Bullying is often an issue for many autistic girls. Ensure that a caring, supportive environment is cultivated and that there are clear policies for reporting and investigating bullying in your setting.

Sensory issues

Sensory sensitivities affect autistic individuals in various ways. Autistic individuals can be over- or under-sensitive to sensory inputs.

Sensory sensitivities

Individuals can have sensitivities with any, or all, of the eight senses listed below. Autistic individuals might be hyper- or hyposensitive. Hypersensitivity means the sensitivity is heightened, for example, if loud noises cause physical pain. Autistic author Laura James describes how hypersensitivity to touch can affect her: 'There are others like me, people who understand how a label in a jumper or a seam on a sock can cause a feeling so distracting everything else fades into the background' (2017, p. 8). Hyposensitivity is when an individual is under-sensitive, for example, an individual who seeks loud noises.

Visual – processing visual information.

Tactile – processing touch and textures.

Auditory – processing noise and sounds.

Gustatory – processing taste and flavour.

Olfactory – processing smells and scent.

Proprioception – relates to where you are in relation to other people and objects, your body awareness.

Vestibular – relating to movement and balance.

Interoception – the sense of what's happening inside your body, such as recognising and identifying bodily sensations such as hunger, thirst, fatigue and temperature.

Being particularly sensitive is more than a simple dislike, but can actually be physically uncomfortable for autistic individuals and often creates a heightened state of anxiety (Wigham et al., 2015). When in this state, attention is focused on trying to eliminate these sensory distractions and many autistic individuals find they are unable to concentrate, learn or communicate, with sensory overload often contributing to meltdowns or shutdowns.

> I wish my teachers or peers knew how distressing it can be when I experience sensory overwhelm. (Sue)

> I can't concentrate on a particular sound (e.g. the teacher's voice). I can always hear the background noise. (Annie, Y7)

> I struggled with bright lights and would sometimes get overwhelmed and snappy at my friends. I didn't understand it as I was not diagnosed. (Autistic female 1)

> After being diagnosed I realise a lot of my issues in school were linked to sensory issues. The unnatural lights were a big issue for me. Also, the background noise of the room was more impactful then I realised and I should've used earplugs. I use them all the time now, especially in public spaces. If I am not allowed to listen to music a simple foam plug really takes away the bulk of the noise and I could just focus on what the teachers were saying. I, similarly to a lot of autistic people, struggled with dyslexia so I had tools such as worksheets printed on blue paper and a blue visor that made it easier for me to read. I also got extra time in exams which helped as it took me longer then my fellow students to process information. (May)

At university – I didn't enjoy group work at all! I always felt like I did not come across as being as intelligent or knowledgeable as the other students and I felt like I was always one step behind with understanding instructions. Also, attending lectures in person felt like a waste of time because I could not keep up (process) what was being said, so I would have to try to learn everything by myself again once I had got home! I found having to sit still through lectures/sessions really difficult, stressful, and uncomfortable. My muscles would seize up and become really painful. Also, anxiety made my stomach sore. Actually, this was my experience all through my education, and because it was my 'normal', I never considered that it could be any different. It was only as an adult, armed with my diagnoses, that I started to advocate for myself, and I realised that it was not normal to sit through classes/lectures without being able to keep up whilst experiencing a lot of discomfort. (Luna)

I was always quiet and well-behaved in school but once I got home, everything would come out – my anger, frustration, irritability, a need to be alone and shut myself off from the world! My parents never understood it at the time (I was undiagnosed). I only later realised how overwhelming everything at school was – the bright lights, the noise, the constant interaction, the crowds, the uncomfortable uniform. I'd hold it all in all day and then explode. (Tori)

I didn't get much work done whilst at university due to distractions so all work completed was at home in my room with zero distractions. (Samantha)

Being sensitive to sensory input can be a particular difficulty in the school environment which is often noisy, crowded and visually overwhelming. Some autistic individuals can have difficulty in filtering out background noise which others find unnoticeable, and for others, noise is amplified.

I can't think and learn in a classroom if there is noise, even if it is just background noise like two teachers talking. (Matilda)

I don't like loud noises; it gets stressful. (Autistic female 5)

The noise and crowds of the school dinner hall were too much for me. (Loz)

I get really annoyed with the people who constantly tap their pens on the table. It's really annoying and means I can't concentrate. Other kids don't even notice it. (Autistic female 13)

Noise! Oh god, how I hated noise. Back in nursery I'd punch, hit, scratch any child that was too loud; I was wild and aggressive at nursery, like a feral animal let loose. Of course in primary school I'd learnt that violence wasn't the answer, but sometimes, if it got too loud … 'Shut up!' I'd scream. I'd cry/moan if a teacher shouted. It didn't matter if two children were fighting – as long as those children fought quietly, who cared if they were seriously injured? There was no need for that teacher to shout. (G)

Meltdowns and shutdowns

When an autistic person becomes completely overwhelmed with their current situation they can experience a meltdown, losing control verbally (shouting, crying, etc.), physically (kicking, lashing out, etc.) or both.

A shutdown appears less obvious to others (an autistic person going quiet or 'switching off') but can be equally debilitating.

These are not 'temper tantrums' but intense and frightening experiences when the sensory system becomes overwhelmed.

Other sensory differences can relate to lighting, taste, smell, clothing and body awareness.

> I don't like walking across the playground because of the pigeons that are there. They fly too close to my head. (Autistic female 5)

> I wish my peers had known how difficult living with sensory issues is – particularly ones that relate to personal hygiene. (Autistic female 8)

> The environment, the noise, lights, fast pace, constant interaction – it was all just chaotic and unmanageable. (Autistic female 10)

> I like having all of the lights on. (Autistic female 13)

> I can't stand bright lights; it makes my eyes feel funny and I can't concentrate. (Tori)

> I hated certain smells too. For example, in primary school I'd always hold my nose when going into the dining room. 'Don't do that, that's rude!' the teachers would say. Why? Why was it rude? It smelt horrible in there, so I had a right to hold my nose, surely? It was only the same as wearing earplugs to a loud job at work. I'd always be the one to point out if someone had let off a bad smell in the classroom too, and I always noticed if a teacher changed her perfume. Certain people I remembered for their smells – there was a girl in secondary school who I knew for her overpowering perfume. I've always loved feeling certain materials as well – I love touching hair, cotton, wool, fluffy dressing gowns etc. but woe betide silk or see-through! I won't wear anything silk or see through, or anything with lots of lace or rough patterning. (G)

> I liked it when we could use the swimming pool in PE but not afterwards. We had to get dry quickly without having a shower or washing our hair. I felt funny for the whole day afterwards and could only think about how itchy my head was because I hadn't been able to wash the chlorine out. (Loz)

Finding lessons was really difficult; I think one class I went to about three times and only then because I happened to follow behind a classmate – I just couldn't find it otherwise. School did not contact parents about such things back then. (Autistic female 32)

I also found the sensory aspect very hard, especially noise. I still constantly request teachers to turn the volume down and complain when bright lights are on. (Autistic female 3)

I couldn't concentrate in lessons (so much input, sensory and social); I couldn't follow the subject matter. (Autistic female 24)

Sensory wise, school got a lot worse in Year 9 on leaving the middle school. Primary and middle school were small and did cause noise problems via the lunch bell and general screaming children, but seemed fairly contained. Secondary on the other hand was big and echoey and had a lot more people in it creating noise that was now more booming voices and girly shrieks. There was also the sudden rush of makeup/perfume/aftershave/deodorant spray smells to deal with alongside the next subject-related smells in chemistry, biology and D&T. There was also a lot more pressure to start breaching uniform rules with skirt lengths, shoes, showing off coloured bras, makeup etc. (Autistic female 33)

Travelling to university classes by train or car to then find parking was a big use of my sensory energy reserves. (Samantha)

Many autistic women learn to cope with their sensory issues by getting to know their individual sensory sensitivities and then managing their environment. Autistic comedian Hannah Gadsby (2022) explains how she copes: 'I leave crowded spaces. I switch off discordant music. I wear headphones at restaurants. I openly express my hatred of the saxophone and electric guitar solos. I don't allow important emotional conversations to take place in cafes with polished concrete floors.' Sensory sensitivities can be particularly difficult to manage at school or college when individuals have little control over their environments and are not in a position to be able to ask for changes to be made. Providing quiet areas for students, as well as making changes in mainstream classrooms and allowing students to suggest helpful individual strategies can all be useful.

I would advise schools to provide a quiet space to hide in, like a sensory room. (Autistic female 13)

I have a 'Leave Early' card so I can leave 3 minutes early from lessons to avoid the rush. (Annie, Y7) (Note from family member: The school has been very flexible and understanding in allowing Annie to have a day off each half term if she's feeling tired and needs a break. For Annie, knowing that she can ask to take the day off occasionally takes the pressure off.)

Ideas for schools

Autistic students are all affected differently by sensory sensitivities. Individuals can be affected more severely when feeling stressed, anxious or tired when tolerance levels can fall, therefore they might be more able to cope with sensory input at some times than others. Get to know your students individually to find out about their specific sensory needs and ensure all staff are aware of these.

Try creating quiet areas for students to work in. Some autistic students find that there is just too much noise in a mainstream classroom for them to concentrate but are able to concentrate better in a quiet area such as school library, quiet room or a study booth which eliminates some of the distractions. Sometimes students can be put off by the stigma attached to doing something that is different to the majority. One way around this is to make quiet spaces open to all, allowing any student to use these as and when needed.

Support students in identifying their needs and the strategies that will work for them. As Abigail Balfe puts it in her book, 'A Different Sort of Normal' (p. 90), 'When experiencing sensory overload, I often need to leave the situation immediately to lie down in a quiet environment alone. But due to people's expectations and how I'm feeling at the time, it can be difficult to make that positive choice for myself'.

Support students to find strategies which work for them as individuals. Some might benefit from wearing ear plugs, others might benefit from sitting in a specific spot in the classroom. Some students might find school uniform extremely uncomfortable so might benefit from ideas such as cutting out labels, buying seamless clothing, wearing a soft layer underneath, wearing specific fabrics, removing items, or wearing their own clothes.

Dimmer switches can be used to create a softer style of lighting in the classroom which may be more comfortable to some students. Natural lighting is usually preferable compared to bright fluorescent lighting. Try turning lights off and opening blinds.

Some sounds that many people hardly notice (such as the hum of the projector or computers) can be overwhelming to those with sensory sensitivities. Simple things, such as switching these off when not in use, can support these students.

The lunch hall can be a particularly difficult environment due to the crowds of people, high volume of noise, lots of movement and various smells. Try creating quieter spaces within the hall or, quieter alternative spaces.

Corridors can be easier to navigate if students keep to one side or follow a one-way system.

> Be aware of visual distractions in the classroom. Too many visual displays can be distracting, as can lots of unnecessary clutter. Keep to the essentials and relevant. This will also help many other students who might have concentration difficulties.
>
> Difficulties with body awareness might create difficulties in practical subjects such as PE, dance, drama and technology, as well as in the classroom. Ensure students have sufficient personal space and give additional time for practical tasks. Avoid leaning over students as this can be uncomfortable for those who need more personal space.

Intense interests

Having a special interest can be a huge source of pleasure and enjoyment for autistic individuals. Often autistic girls have interests similar to those of their non-autistic peers; the difference – what makes it a 'special', or intense interest – is often the intensity and dominance of the interest. It is not just a hobby or interest, but it takes over other aspects of their life.

Whereas autistic boys might stand out because of an unusual interest, girls' special interests may not seem anything out of the ordinary – they might be interested in horses, celebrities or a soap opera, for example (Simone, 2010). However, in comparison with their peers, they will approach this interest with phenomenal intensity, perhaps planning their lives around the interests and keeping fact files, catalogues or lists of information about the subject.

> I had a huge knowledge of my special interests. (Autistic female 11)
>
> I was hugely interested in anything to do with the environment. (Autistic female 12)
>
> The school exchange trip to Germany was a real highlight. (Autistic female 10)
>
> I had a huge in-depth knowledge of my special interest and could talk about it for hours. I knew lots of facts, and it was where I focused my energy and attention. (Autistic female 25)
>
> I got a lot of joy from my special interest which was socially acceptable – horse riding. (Autistic female 1)

In the school environment, special interests may have a positive as well as negative impact. If a special interest links with a particular subject area, it could lead to students excelling in that subject area. Having a special interest may also lead to success in extracurricular activities and help to increase an individual's confidence and self-esteem. For some students, however, a special interest can mean they are distracted from the learning required in school.

Being good at music and languages helped my self-esteem. (LJ)

My special interest was Coronation Street. I wouldn't miss an episode, read everything I could about it and had watched all the past episodes I could get my hands on. I learned everything I could about the characters' histories and backgrounds. I had a huge amount of factual knowledge about it (the number of episodes each character had appeared in etc.). I built a routine around watching it and would not go out on those evenings and would get hugely anxious if it looked like something was going to get in the way of watching it. I built a scale model of the set. I taped every episode on to video cassette and catalogued these, rewatching the scenes with my favourite characters. I felt that these characters were my friends. I would get really quite frustrated with classmates who claimed they also liked watching it, as they just weren't interested in talking about it in the amount of detail I was. They knew nothing. As an adult I look back and it seems such a waste of time. However, at the time, it was my world. Looking back, I acquired a lot of skills through this special interest – how to use a VCR, research skills, cataloguing, learning, understanding people. (Tori)

Spending time engaged with a special interest can be a time of relaxation for autistic individuals and can help to reduce anxiety, taking the individual away from the confusion of real life and into a world they are in control of. There can, however, be problems too. Some autistic girls can become so engrossed with their special interest that the real world becomes meaningless and less attractive in comparison. Others may find it difficult to switch their attention or might only want to talk about their special interest. Others, with more unusual interests, might find that they become a source of amusement or teasing to their peers.

Many autistic students report excelling at a certain subject, especially if this happens to link with their special interest, for example, languages, reading, the environment or music. In these cases, many girls and women report having a wide and in-depth knowledge of their special interest and being able to focus for extended periods on these interests. Perhaps surprisingly, however, this is sometimes not seen as a positive in the classroom environment.

I knew more than the teachers about medieval history, which was my special interest from a young age. I got very frustrated in history lessons because I didn't feel challenged. I had a huge amount of knowledge, but often this wasn't recognised in school where the focus was simply on learning what you had to know for the exam. No extra credit is given for knowing things not specified on the syllabus. (Autistic female 21)

I knew a lot about my special interests and used to correct the teachers; this did not always go down well! (Autistic female 25)

My special interests were drama and psychology which I was lucky enough to study, meaning I had an excuse to talk about and research my special interests. (May)

> ### Ideas for schools
>
> A special interest can be a good way to learn new skills (e.g. research skills, literacy) and to increase self-esteem. Support students to recognise the skills they are developing through their special interest. Some students might also be able to pursue a career related to their special interest – if this is relevant, help them to research and plan this. It can help increase motivation.
>
> Some autistic girls can find it beneficial to find others with similar interests, as this can be an easier way of making friends and communicating with others. There might be extra-curricular groups in or outside of school (e.g. Lego clubs, reading groups).
>
> Talking about a special interest might be a way to start to build a professional relationship with the individual in question.

Feelings and emotions

Difficulties with recognising and understanding feelings (both in self and in others) is one of the main characteristics of autism. There can be difficulties with labelling feelings, understanding why they and others feel the way that they do, expressing emotions, distinguishing between your own and other people's emotions, and managing feelings. Some autistic individuals also react to other people's emotions differently than is typically expected – some might not know how to react, or might react 'inappropriately', for example, laughing when they do not understand the situation.

> ### Alexithymia
>
> Difficulties understanding and describing one's own emotions is known as alexithymia. It is more common in autistic individuals than in non-autistic individuals (Autistica, 2022). Alexithymia can make it difficult for autistic people to regulate their emotions and can worsen anxiety.

Many autistic individuals report being overwhelmed by feelings such as anxiety, nervousness or loneliness, which can have a long-lasting negative impact on all aspects of life. Before diagnosis, it is also common for autistic individuals to feel 'different', on a different wavelength or like they don't fit in.

> I felt that nobody recognised how I was feeling. Well-meaning comments like 'You'll be fine' and 'Everybody feels like that sometimes' showed that people didn't really understand.

> Things that were important to other people weren't important to me. People kept telling me what I should be aiming for or people seemed to have a preconceived idea of what must be important to me, but it just wasn't. I didn't feel that I was the same as others. I was different and didn't fit in. (Tori)

> I feel lonely and like I don't belong here. (Loz)

> I used to read my way through the psychology section of the local library, trying to find out what was wrong with me. (Autistic female 11)

> I hated it when people assumed what I was feeling. 'Oh, you must be feeling so upset' when I wasn't upset at all. (Matilda)

> I never fitted in. I remember getting teased and bullied a lot and being incredibly tearful most of the time. I just wasn't happy. (Autistic female 10)

> I was always bursting into tears at school, which was pretty awful. (Autistic female 12)

> People didn't seem to understand why some things were important to me. Telling me 'not to worry' or to 'just forget about it' was no help at all. I just felt even more misunderstood. (Tori)

> School is a pressured structure, and there is no time or space to bounce back from upsets. We need this time and space. (Autistic female 24)

Some autistic women identified that their difficulties and emotions often went unnoticed due to them having generally appropriate social skills and appearing to be able to communicate effectively on the surface.

> We female Aspies are usually a little more expressive in face and gesture than male Aspies; we can mirror many different types of personalities better than male Aspies, so we usually don't have a strong sense of identity, even before diagnosis. More so than male Aspies, we are a little more open to talking about our feelings and emotions. We appear more adept than boys and men with AS, so we usually receive less tolerance, and expectations from others are high. We usually give the appearance that we're skilled at socialising, but in actuality, it's a 'performance'. We're good at socialising in small doses, but like males with AS, we'll shut down when overloaded. (Autistic female 34)

Others found that their feelings, emotions and empathy were ignored or unnoticed because of a lack of facial expression. As Abilgail Balfe expresses in her book 'A Different Sort of Normal' (2021, p. 63) – 'You see… just because I am not always openly displaying an emotion, doesn't mean I'm not feeling an emotion.' And as Charlotte Amelia Poe explains in How to be Autistic (2019, p. 28): 'I really do believe that people don't understand that just because we freeze up around emotion doesn't mean we don't feel it, or know that you're suffering. We just don't know what to do with that information. Which can be tricky.'

Some autistic women report that misunderstanding other people's intentions or feelings caused upset.

> I am very honest and reliable. I always saw the good in everybody. This has led to me being hurt, but I still see it as a positive. (Autistic female 24)

On the positive side, some autistic women felt their own experiences meant they were able to empathise with others who were vulnerable or 'different'.

> I was kind to people who were pushed out for reasons I was unaware of. (Autistic female 12)

There's a stereotype that autistic people lack empathy but this isn't true for many. Some feel that the difficulty is that they can't express the empathy they feel. Others feel they are too empathetic, that they are empaths who feel other people's emotions acutely. Charlotte Amelia Poe, in How to be Autistic (2019, p. 27), describes it as 'The problem is an excess, if anything, of empathy. We feel your anger, your pain, your sadness. And then we overload and don't know how to handle that.' Some autistic individuals find they are unable to separate other people's emotions from their own – they pick up and absorb emotions from those around them: 'Like many autistic people, I am an empath. Although I sometimes find it difficult to identify my own emotions, I feel other people's moods, emotions and energy on a deep level. I will often absorb the feelings of whoever I am with.' – Abigail Balfe in 'A Different Sort of Normal' (p. 60).

> Class discussions becoming ridiculous or heated would make me feel anxious and angry. (Samantha)

> Sometimes I'd go into lessons feeling fine but come out feeling 'funny', a feeling I couldn't accurately describe at the time. I guess a mix of anxious, irritable, overwhelmed and stressed. Often it was lessons when others had been misbehaving or if somebody had been emotional. I remember one incident when I was in primary school. A girl had been very upset, missing her mum. I was anxious and 'off' for the rest of the day. It's only as I've got older I realise I somehow pick up on other people's emotions and can't separate them from my own. I think that is what was happening. (Autistic female 11)

Bullying

Many autistic students report being bullied or teased during their time at school. Some say that they feel vulnerable because of their differences, isolation and the lack of a supportive friendship group. Others feel that they are not necessarily bullied but simply left out, as others do not find them easy to engage with. Some perceived bullying, for example, when their preferences were not respected and not taken seriously ('You can't really want to stay on your own! Come and play with us.'), or when they were constantly being forced into a box they were not meant to fit in, yet found others did not consider this to be bullying.

> A lot of the time, we can see the neurotypical person as a bully. It's understandable because whether or not they know it, they're forcing us into a box that we simply were not meant to fit in, so it's like we aren't good enough until we give the performance or impression of 'normal' 24/7. Even the neurotypicals who come to understand us or know a decent amount about Asperger's sometimes give the impression that they want to change us for good. (Autistic female 35)
> Depression from bullying and social misfitting is a bigger deal than it's made out to be, especially if a student has anything else going on. I was so close to dying from depression, and I don't think anyone knew how close. (Autistic female 36)

A lack of assertiveness and self-esteem, along with difficulties understanding others' points of view can also create the feeling of being bullied.

> There was a group of girls chatting in the corridor, and I wanted to get past. I wasn't confident enough to ask them to let me through. They didn't even seem to notice I was standing there wanting to get past. I thought they were bullying me. (Loz)

Some autistic students can find it difficult to identify whether or not they are being bullied or begin to doubt their interpretation of the situation because of their previous experiences of being told they are in the wrong. Abigail Balfe, in 'A Different Sort of Normal' (p. 141) explains why she didn't report being bullied: 'I found talking [...] challenging, so I wasn't going to start a conversation on a difficult subject with an adult when I couldn't be sure I really needed to. I didn't trust my own judgement. I didn't think I was being bullied 'properly' or 'enough'... So I just left it.'

Ideas for schools

Many autistic students want to learn from what has happened. Support them to unpick situations in a neutral and non-judgemental way. Help them to consider what other people may have been thinking, feeling or expecting. Help others to consider the situation from an autistic point of view.

Many autistic females report being bookworms who enjoyed being in the school library or escaping into worlds of fiction. There is evidence that reading has many positive effects such as reducing depression (Fanner & Urquart, 2008; Cuijpers, 1997; Den Boer et al., 2004), enhancing theory of mind (Kidd & Castano, 2013) and increasing satisfaction with life (Book Trust, 2013). Added benefits for autistic girls can be the opportunity to enjoy solitude and

> quietness (often needed to recover after social contact) and gain a better insight into the thoughts, feelings and actions of others. There's an increasing number of children and young adult novels available written by female autistic authors containing autistic protagonists. This can help autistic students see similar characters to themselves in books, and help neurotypical students to understand neurodivergent classmates. Stocking a range of these books in the classroom or school library can be helpful for all students. A list of some of these books is included in the Further Resources section.
>
> Some autistic students need the time and space to bounce back from everyday incidents and misunderstandings. Ensure that there are quiet places to go when students feel overwhelmed and staff available to help talk through issues if wanted.
>
> Support students to access support from qualified counsellors and therapists when needed. Autistic students benefit from therapists who are trained specifically in working with neurodivergent individuals.
>
> Be aware that autistic students are often experiencing a wide range of emotions – but sometimes they might not express these in the expected neurotypical ways.
>
> Autistic students might need help in identifying how they are feeling. However, be careful not to impose neurotypical expectations (e.g. 'You must feel so lonely here by yourself' – actually the student might be enjoying their own company) and try not to dismiss the students' feelings as 'wrong' (e.g. 'You shouldn't feel angry about that') as this can contribute to the individual learning not to accept their feelings as okay.

Anxiety and absence from school

Anxiety

Anxiety can be common in autistic individuals. Research suggests that anxiety is more common in autistic individuals than in neurotypicals (van Steensel et al., 2011; Lugnegård et al., 2011) and that anxiety in autistic individuals can have a significant impact on their quality of life. One survey of autistic women found that over 80% considered themselves to experience anxiety, worry or stress frequently (Baldwin & Costley, 2015).

Some of the reasons for increased feelings of anxiety can include:

- Sensory overwhelm causing heightened anxiety
- Difficulty in reading other people's emotions – not being able to predict how others might react. This can make social situations anxiety-provoking

- Not being able to understand one's own emotions and feeling overwhelmed by these
- The constant pressure of have to 'mask' or pretend to fit in to meet social expectations
- Difficulties coping with uncertainty and change
- Having difficulty in communicating with others – perhaps often feeling dismissed or misunderstood
- Fear of failure
- The difficulties and pressure that come from living in a world designed for neurotypical people

Some autistic individuals might not be able to identify that they are anxious themselves (because of difficulties interpreting their emotions, or even because this has become their 'default' setting), and others might respond to anxiety in different ways than neurotypicals. For example, in one research study (Joyce et al., 2017), autistic young people and adults reported that when they are anxious they might become more repetitive in their actions, might spend more time on hobbies and interests and might become more insistent on set routines. Researchers have recently begun to develop assessment methods designed specifically to identify anxiety in autistic adults and young people, for example the Anxiety Scale for Children – ASD (Rodgers, 2016).

Stimming

Stimming is short for 'self-stimulating behaviours' and is often associated with autism. Stimming can include repetitive actions or behaviours such as physical movements (e.g. hand-flapping, rocking, jumping, spinning or twirling), or repetitive use of objects or of the senses (e.g. repeatedly feeling a particular texture, or twirling a piece of string). Autistic people might stim to cope with sensory overload, to cope with anxiety, or when they are bored. Some individuals stim to gain or reduce sensory input.

I was undiagnosed and also did not know I was dyslexic so I would often burn myself out trying too hard to complete tests, study and revise. Not knowing my limits and struggling with interoception, I massively let my health slip during high school. I struggled with depression as well as the constant anxiety. Only until I got into college and started prioritising my needs did I understand how much I was affected by school. (May)

At school, there is so much that I disliked that it's hard to pick out even a couple of things. Overall, I didn't know things could be any better, so I just had to get on with it and anxiety/stress were my 'norm'. I had very little support or understanding from teachers and got into trouble on quite a few occasions for, for example, 'refusing' to speak. (Luna)

> I felt anxious all of the time. I felt I had no real friends and break and lunchtimes were awful – I would hide in the toilets or sit in a classroom as the canteen was too noisy and smelly, and I had nobody to sit with. I was incredibly shy and quiet in class and always worrying about being asked a question or what we would do next. I worried about everything, and others always seemed to know things that I didn't, even though I always listened to everything the teachers said and read all the information we were given. It was a real mystery! (Matilda)

> I always needed to feel prepared to reduce anxiety. I would do a lot of research to prepare so I could contribute something but then others would think I was showing off or trying to show them up. (Autistic female 11)

> I developed C-PTSD partly due to bullying for the way I was. It's incredibly draining to have to socialise and work whilst fighting off things nobody can see. To every autistic person being bullied or with PTSD, keep going. You are way stronger than that. (Autistic female 3)

Some autistic individuals find they put into places routines, structures and timetables to help them to reduce anxiety and unpredictability.

> I loved the routine of having a timetable. (Tori)

> I also liked having a routine and knowing what was expected. (Autistic female 10)

> I like well-structured lessons. (Autistic female 13)

> I liked the structure of school, knowing what was going to happen next and feeling prepared. (Autistic female 11)

> I liked having a uniform – always loved knowing exactly what I was wearing, what I was supposed to wear every day! (Autistic female 12)

> Routines were a massive part of my ASD, and still are – being late would stress me out. It still does. Woe betide the teachers if lessons ran five minutes over what they were meant to or if break ended five minutes early. (G)

Selective mutism

Selective mutism is an anxiety disorder where a person is unable to speak in certain situations, such as in a classroom or around people they do not know very well. Many individuals dislike the term 'selective' as it implies they are choosing not to talk. For individuals in this situation the stress, anxiety and sensory overload make speaking aloud impossible. Autistic comedian Hannah Gadsby (2022) explains how it affects her: 'I often lose my verbal ability. Especially if I am overwhelmed by a lot of sensory information at the same time as I am trying to identify, process and regulate emotional distress. This is what is called selective mutism.'

Selective mutism can affect anybody and usually begins in early childhood, around the ages of two to four. It is also more common in girls and in migrant and multi-lingual families (SMIRA, 2023). Selective mutism is also thought to be common in autistic individuals.

Absence from school

Anxiety can often be the main contributing factor to absence from school (or 'school refusal' as it is often described) in autistic young people. This anxiety can stem from a number of challenges in the school environment (i.e. sensory overload, difficulties with learning, bullying, friendship difficulties, difficulties communicating, being misunderstood, difficulty coping with changes to routine and finding social times difficult). Absence from school can be extremely difficult for the student, family and school staff. In some cases it can be difficult to identify the source of anxiety about school if the autistic student isn't able to identify or articulate this herself. Parents can feel pressured to get their child back into school, which causes further difficulties.

Ideas for schools

Ensure professionals supporting autistic students, including therapists, mentors, Education Welfare Officers and attendance officers, have a good understanding of autism. Some strategies used with other students might need to be adapted for use with autistic students who have difficulty with alexithymia and who interpret the world differently.

It might take time to identify why individual autistic students are no longer happy to attend school. Some students might not be able to identify these reasons themselves. Reasons might be different to neurotypical students – for example, sensory issues might play a greater role.

Individual solutions will need to be found for each student. Some will benefit from specialist therapy from a qualified psychotherapist. Some students benefit from a flexible approach, perhaps combining time in school with online tuition or home tutoring, or from being taught on a one-to-one or small-group basis.

Avoid creating further anxiety for the student. They are already experiencing significant difficulties, and adding pressure to attend school, or putting this pressure on to parents, can worsen the situation. Some students might be able to keep up academically (e.g. learning from home or with a private tutor) while they get support for any underlying issues.

> Communicate with students absent from school and ensure they have the opportunity to stay involved with their learning, whatever form this might take.
>
> Changes in the classroom or school routine might help some students, for example, environmental changes to reduce sensory input, being able to spend social times in a quiet area, or staff communicating in a different way.
>
> Seek professional support for selective mutism from a Speech and Language Therapist or Mental Health Professional. Advice is often based on avoiding further stress by not demanding the individual speaks – instead encourage communication in whatever other form the individual is able to.

Self-esteem and masking

Self-esteem is often described as the discrepancy between the 'ideal self' and our self-image (McGirl, 2009). Levels of self-esteem are often a reflection of a combination of factors – things that can contribute include parental/community/cultural attitudes, societal expectations, the influence of the media and social media, our early experiences, educational experiences, our relationships with others, and other life events. In other words, self-esteem can be seen as a 'cumulative record of how we have been treated and how we treat ourselves' (Atkinson & Hornby, 2002). Our self-esteem encompasses the beliefs and feelings we have about our competence and self-worth, our beliefs that we can confront challenges and move out of our comfort zone (McGirl, 2009).

Self-esteem is often seen as a vital ingredient for personal success and happiness. Although low self-esteem affects many individuals in the general population, it can be particularly prevalent among autistic individuals. There is evidence, for example, that female autistic adolescents perceive themselves as having lower social competence, lower self-worth and a lower quality of life than their more typically developing peers, while non-autism groups rate themselves higher across all aspects of social-emotional health (Jamison & Schuttler, 2015). Many factors might contribute to this, such as experiencing negative reactions from others, being compared to others unfavourably, not understanding why they are different – or having a diagnosis which they feel labels them, feeling the constant need to mask, and having their natural preferences, thoughts and behaviours deemed odd or inferior in the media and wider society. Sara Gibbs, in 'Drama Queen' (2021, p. 2) explains the effect of being undiagnosed had on her self-esteem: 'Until I was thirty years old I thought I was the most uniquely terrible person in the world. Nobody in existence was as selfish, lazy, incapable, weak, dramatic, inappropriate, ridiculous or out of sync with the world as I was.'

> If I could go back to my old school and speak to my teachers, I would want them to know that their negative attitudes towards me resulted in a lifetime of anxiety, depression, and chronic illness. Overall, I would say that they were completely wrong on their assumptions of me and how I experienced the world. (Autistic female 25)

> Coming out of education (especially school) with good self-esteem is much more important than coming out with a handful of qualifications. The damage that is done to self-esteem in a person's formative years can lead to a lifetime of poor mental health and lack of fulfilment, which are very hard to overcome in adulthood. I know this from experience as I spent my 20s and 30s believing that I was unintelligent and incapable of achieving anything. In my late 30s I returned to academic study and with the proper support I was able to achieve both my bachelor's and master's degrees with distinctions. However, despite my achievements and finally believing that I am intelligent, I still continue to battle with low self-esteem, which impacts on all aspects of my life. (Luna)

Some students feel they have inner confidence in themselves and their abilities but that this isn't recognised by others, perhaps due to how they come across in terms of their facial expression, body language or ability to communicate.

> I feel confident about my ability to do things, but other people don't seem to see this (probably because of my quietness and lack of expression), so I wasn't given opportunities that would have been good for me, like being a prefect. (Matilda)

Being shy or quiet led to several girls feeling that they were 'invisible' or 'unnoticed' by staff and peers, which again had a negative impact on self-esteem.

> Autistic girls can simply appear incredibly shy and quiet – which doesn't seem particularly unusual, and may mean that they are overlooked because they aren't outwardly displaying any problems – they can be 'invisible'. (Autistic female 11)

> I faced a lot of assumptions of laziness growing up when I was burning myself out trying too hard. Giving children the benefit of the doubt, believing them and helping search for solutions is an attitude all teachers should have. Even if a child may not be diagnosed at the time you have no idea what really is going on in their heads, chances are they're as frustrated as you that they can't cope. As for environmental changes, more natural lighting where possible! Even for neurotypical people this would help so much with learning. But my main point is more focus on the quiet kid! It's true what they say it's the quiet kids you should look out for. The ones who pass by with enough good grades and are well behaved, may be the ones who are struggling the most. My mother fought a lot to get teachers to recognise how much I was struggling because she saw the meltdowns as soon as I got home. But because I was a bright kid who tried hard and kept her head down they never bothered to try to help or change anything. By the

time I'd stop trying and my grades dropped it was too late. So my advice to teachers would be if a parent or child says they're struggling, when you think they're doing fine, believe them. (May)

Often it is the expectations of the 'neurotypical' world that create the difficulties and affect self-esteem negatively.

I feel confident in my own world but not in this one. (Loz)

For some, their ways of coping with their negative feelings and low self-esteem caused further problems: Some truanted regularly, missed out on education or developed long-lasting problems such as self-harming or eating disorders.

Feeling misunderstood by staff and peers can also cause difficulties:

There seems to be no recognition from staff that they and their expectations create pressure. The unwilling, belligerent child facing you and being 'encouraged' could be a distressed child being 'bullied'. (Autistic female 37)

There was autism awareness for the other kids in school, but it was horrible. I am nothing like the people in the video they showed, and it made it sound like there was something terrible wrong with me. I didn't want the other kids to know about my autism after that. (Loz)

I don't want others to treat me as if I am disabled or lack intelligence. I don't want them to pity me. I just want to be treated equally but as an individual. (Autistic female 12)

Not fully being able to express one's self or what one is expressing can also lead to low self-esteem, as autistic comedian Hannah Gadsby (2022) explains: 'During my adolescence I began to find it more and more difficult to make myself understood, and that is when I developed an instinctive habit of taking the blame whenever I didn't understand what was going on around me – which, to be clear, was all the time.'

Masking

The term 'masking' is often used to describe how autistic individuals try to fit in, by masking, camouflaging or hiding their true selves in order to fit into a neurotypical world. This pretending to be somebody else can be conscious or subconscious and can take many forms: suppressing behaviours that others might think are strange; copying others' body language and communication style; or developing 'scripts' to get by in social situations. Masking can be exhausting and can contribute to mental health difficulties (Bradley et al., 2021; Hull et al., 2017). Autistic individuals who mask might not even be aware of what they are doing, but they

> can be exhausted from trying so hard to fit in to a world not designed for them, and can lose sense of their own identity. Autistic writer Laura James in her autobiography 'Odd Girl Out' (2017, p. 31) explains how she 'masked' as a child: 'I had no idea how to think and feel like everybody else, so instead, I tried to look like them, dress like them and – weirdly important to my seven-year-old self – to acquire similar possessions to those they owned.'

Masking

Conversations always seemed to go wrong without me knowing why. I'd say something that I'd heard others say or that I thought was the 'right' thing to say because I never knew what to say myself. But then people would question me or disagree with me and I'd be horrified because I actually agreed with them, I'd only said whatever it was to try and fit in. It took me a long time to realise what I was doing. (Tori)

I wish my peers had known there was a lot going on in my head that I couldn't communicate to them – anxieties, worries, fears, indecision, rumination. I knew I was different but I couldn't explain to them how. I was doing a lot of pretending. (Matilda)

As I was undiagnosed throughout my education, I found the social element hardest. I was held to the same social standards as my neurotypical peers and humiliated numerous times by both teachers and students if I didn't meet them. Things I most struggled with included: crowded corridors, bright lights, speaking in class and the chronic fatigue and mental health struggles I experienced as a result of masking. (Alis)

I wish my teachers and peers knew about autistic masking. I believe if my teachers had, then they'd have taken my concerns more seriously under the understanding that my external expressions and appearance were not a representation of my mental state. Even in the most drastic circumstances where I was experiencing anxiety attacks or severe depression, teachers noted that I seemed calm and passive, therefore believing my experience was over dramatic or even false. Additionally, if my peers had understood, I believe they would've been more at ease with my presence, understanding how I seemed so different amongst my close friends than how I was in classrooms. I was bullied at times during my education for my autistic traits, if others had more acceptance of differences then this wouldn't have occurred. (Alis)

I found it very difficult to express my feelings and the level of distress and anxiety I felt. I still find that difficult, even with health professionals, friends and family. It takes a lot for me to be able to drop the mask, and masking is so exhausting. I end up thinking that nobody would like the real me, that I am too difficult or demanding. (Sue)

Some autistic girls experience an intense pressure to 'fit in' or to be 'normal'. At the same time, some can recognise they are somehow 'different' and need something different than their peers. Their desire just to be 'normal' can, however, be overwhelming, and they do not want anything that would make them seem more different than they already are.

> I needed something different but at the same time didn't want to be treated any different as it would have just made me feel even more 'odd'. (Autistic female 10)

Benefits of diagnosis

Not all autistic people choose to pursue a diagnosis. There can be a stigma about neurodivergent conditions or a lack of autism awareness in some communities. Others might feel a formal diagnosis will make little difference to their everyday lives. However, there can be many benefits of formal diagnosis. Individuals might:

- Feel they finally have an explanation for the difficulties and differences they have experienced. This new awareness can help them understand why previous misunderstandings or negative experiences have occurred.

- Now be able to access the support or services they need in order to succeed in education, employment and everyday life.

- Feel others are more accepting of their differences if they have a formal diagnosis.

- Feel a diagnosis has a positive impact on their mental health. The validation of a formal diagnosis can mean that some feel less of a need to mask and are more able to self-advocate for what they need. They might gain in self-awareness and self-compassion, and improve their sense of self-identity. For example, Sara Gibbs, in 'Drama Queen' (2021, p. 324) explains the change in perspective she experienced: 'I had spent my whole life trying to fit in and be like everybody else. I had wasted thirty years of my life trying to achieve something that was far beyond my reach instead of letting myself be comfortable with who I was.'

- Find similar people through online or face-to-face support groups which helps them feel a sense of self-belonging.

Implications for schools – There can be long waiting lists for autism diagnoses in some parts of the country, however, that does not mean that effective and appropriate support cannot be put into place in the meantime. Help should be based on need, not on diagnosis. Many helpful strategies will help all students, and will not harm students, should they end up with a different, or no, diagnosis. For example, allowing all students who need

> it access to a quiet area, will help those undiagnosed/not yet diagnosed students, as well as reduce any stigma related to accessing something that is 'different'. Waiting until a formal diagnosis happens (which can take years in some areas currently) might be too late for some students whose mental health, self-esteem and enjoyment of school might have deteriorated significantly in that period.

What helps to promote self-esteem? Some autistic girls report enjoying and benefitting from opportunities in which they were able to play to their strengths or feel good about themselves.

> I like teachers who don't embarrass me. (Autistic female 5)

> I like having responsibility given to me, like collecting the registers. (LJ)

> I loved music and was involved with orchestra and wind band. Being good at these things increased my self-esteem. (Luna)

> I was smart and that allowed me to be in a safe class. I felt seen as teachers made me feel good for being smart. (Autistic female 1)

> Be patient; be kind; try to understand when we say we don't understand; explain it differently without making us feel bad about ourselves. Tell us when we've done something well. Make us feel good about being us. (G)

> Writing my own story has helped me a lot with my confidence. I take advice from what I've learned in the past. (Loz)

And is there any advice autistic women would give to staff to help others like them improve their self-esteem and wellbeing?

> I think an understanding of how autistic people differ and how their learning needs are different is necessary. I also think educational staff should teach in ways that people understand, and stop the one size fits all. (Autistic female 2)

> Understand that ability changes hour to hour; just because someone could do something once doesn't mean they are not trying if they cannot again. Make us feel good about ourselves; help us to accept this is the way we are and that is how other people are. Show us why misunderstandings have occurred without judging us. (Autistic female 12)

> Allow us to have our own goals, targets and hopes, not ones that have been imposed by school or other people. (Autistic female 11)

Get to know them [autistic students] as individuals rather than assume that all autistic students want or need the same things. Support them with their interests and passions and create opportunities around those. Be ambitious for their futures! Find autistic (and other neurodivergent) role models! (Autistic female 24)

There is a lot of overlap between autism and ADHD, as well as between autism and other types of neurodiversity (dyspraxia, dyslexia, etc.). I think it's rare to have just autism and not fit the criteria for at least one other diagnosis. Furthermore, none of these 'labels' really tell you who a person is or their strengths and weaknesses, etc., as most people do not fit the stereotypical profiles. Therefore, it is important to get to know each student's unique profile. (LJ)

Ideas for schools

Don't try to force autistic students to be 'less autistic' or 'more normal'. This is exhausting and confusing. Rather, encourage self-esteem and support students to identify their strengths. Be aware that 'masking' can take a tremendous amount of energy. Masking can be conscious or subconscious.

Ensure that accessible support is available for autistic students and that this support is discreet and does not add to their feelings of being different. Some students might dislike the stigma of having an assistant sit next to them in lessons, for example. Open up any extra resources (e.g. quiet rooms) to all students who need them to remove any stigma attached.

Ensure any autism-awareness activities give an accurate and positive view of autism. Some autistic girls may not identify with the more usual portrayals of autism in the media (often based on males with learning and language disabilities). This can lead to them feeling even more misunderstood or that they have been misrepresented. Include autistic individuals in the planning of any awareness activities. Be aware of the language that is used in your setting relating to neurodiversity and disabilities.

Transition

Transition to new settings

Major transitions can be a difficult time for any student, not just autistic students. Transition from primary school to secondary school, from secondary school to college or simply from one year group to other can be a time of confusion and unpredictability – new teachers, new classrooms, new classmates, new rules, routines and expectations.

Transition between primary and secondary school can be especially difficult for autistic girls. Secondary schools are often much larger and students go from having had one teacher in one classroom, to having many different teachers and classrooms. There's also a great deal more expected in terms of independence and self-organisation.

> The primary school and class sizes were very small which probably helped, and there were only four classes in the whole school which meant very little transition or change. (Matilda)

> A new school, new buildings, new teachers, new students, new routines – new everything! God, this was terrifying! (Georgia)

> I liked having the smaller classes in primary school and getting the one-to-one time with teachers. (LJ)

The transition to college or university and beyond can also pose challenges and opportunities. Some autistic students enjoy the freedom of college and university – the fact that there is less expectation to fit in is often a benefit. Some find the increased independence difficult.

> At sixth form I had to resit maths four or five times and was pretty rubbish at A levels: I couldn't pay attention. I had a great social life there though; I met the alternative crowd, finally people who were more like me. (Autistic female 38)

> I went to university but wasn't ready. I couldn't cope. I lasted a year and failed completely. (Autistic female 10)

> Sixth form college was great as the pupils who messed about weren't there, and it was a more grown-up and sensible environment. I worried incessantly about what to do when I left school – the thought of having to choose optional subjects, which degree and university and then which career was just overwhelming. (Matilda)

> I loved the academic side of university but living in halls of residence was a complete disaster. The noise! The people! The constant bombardment! The constant having to try hard to appear normal! I dropped out of university because of this and it destroyed the little self-esteem I had. (Tori)

Is there any advice autistic women would give to their younger counterparts about transition to further education and beyond?

> Think about your personality – likes and dislikes and your skills; is there something you would like to do as a career or hobby, something you can enjoy and be good at? That way it won't feel like work. (Autistic female 25)

Be wary about making your special interest your career – it can leave you with nothing to do outside of work, and you may end up hating/resenting it ultimately because it becomes something you no longer love but are forced to do as employment. (Autistic female 19)

If you go to university, let the university know about your autism and how you study best; ask for accommodation that suits you, house shares don't work for everyone – a room of your own away from noisy areas may work well, or go to a local university. Seek out clubs and societies to meet like-minded people. (Autistic female 10)

Think about the environment you find soothing/stimulating and which would be best for you to learn in. (LJ)

Daily transitions

It's not only these major transitions that autistic students can find difficult. Transitions happen throughout the day – the transition from 'being at home' to 'being in school', the transition from studying one subject to studying another, the transition from lessons to social times, the transition back from school to home. These transition times can sometimes be a trigger for shutdowns or meltdowns in the school environment.

Some autistic students have difficulty in shifting their attention from one task to another, or in shifting from one state of mind (e.g. 'I'm at home relaxing') to another ('Now I'm focusing on Maths'), or are unable to start one task until they've completed another. They might be unable to focus on the new task as they are unable to get the unfinished task out of their mind.

Ideas for schools

The ability to cope with change can change on a day-to-day basis for autistic students, depending on anxiety levels and self-esteem.

Transitions from one activity to another can be times that autistic students find difficult. Having clear transition times and routines might help (for example, on arrival at school, after social times). Some students will also benefit from unhurried transitions from one activity to the next in the classroom and from being given the opportunity to complete tasks before moving on to a new subject.

The transition to secondary school can be particularly difficult for some autistic students. Extra support might include having additional visits to the new setting prior to starting, being visited by staff from the new setting in their current setting, having a mentor in the new setting and being given clear information about timetables and expectations.

> Ensure that staff in new settings, and new staff coming into a setting – such as substitute teachers – are made aware of students' needs and the strategies that are needed. Sharing pupil profiles can be one way of doing this. Involve students in the creation of pupil profiles.
>
> Unstructured times such as breaks and lunchtimes can be particularly challenging when somewhere new. Support students in advance to know what their options are.
>
> Autistic students might require more support than others in choosing an appropriate course of further study or route to employment. They might benefit from support in identifying how their autism may affect them in future situations.

Puberty, gender and sexuality

Puberty

Of course, puberty and growing up is something all young people experience, and many have difficulties with, but there can be some specific challenges for autistic girls. Change and uncertainty can be particularly difficult for autistic individuals, and the physical and emotional changes of puberty can be particularly unpredictable – the physical changes with body shape, the start of menstruation, bodily hair, and the hormonal impact on mood and attitude. Autistic girls might also lack a tight friendship group with which to discuss these issues, compared with their neurotypical peers who might find comfort and understanding in realising they are not alone in what is happening to them. In addition, these physical and hormonal changes often coincide with the transition from primary school to secondary school, and with the time when girls' friendships suddenly become more complicated. Friends who they used to play with, now just want to chat – often about their feelings, or about other people, or about relationships. Autistic girls might start to realise that they are 'different' from their peers, and that these differences might not be seen as a positive thing.

> Puberty and secondary schooling was a very bad combination. Learning whilst enduring some of the weirdest changes in life was impossible. Every preference I made was due to puberty and being autistic with no idea what was going on. The social pressure was immense. (Samantha)

> Puberty was the worst time. I felt nobody was experiencing what I was. It was just awful. The monthly bleeding and accompanying pain. Feeling totally embarrassed about using sanitary products. Feeling totally embarrassed about my whole body, my breasts, my changing shape, spots on my chin that I just couldn't hide. I was too embarrassed to talk about it to anybody. (Matilda)

Sensory issues can also play a role. As Abigail Balfe describes in 'A Different Sort of Normal' (2021): 'Wearing a pad may not feel comfortable, especially if you are sensitive to sensory stimuli like I am. And the idea of putting something like a tampon or a Mooncup inside yourself might feel scary.'

There is some evidence which suggests that autistic females might be more affected by hormonal changes too. Some studies suggest that autistic and ADHD females might be disproportionately affected by PMDD (Pre-menstrual Dysphoric Disorder) than other populations (Obaydi et al., 2008). Some possible suggestions that have been made include autistic females' sensory sensitivities might contribute to this, or that autistic females might be more sensitive to hormones, though more research is needed in this area (ADDitude, 2022).

Gender issues

One of the biggest difficulties that many autistic females report is feeling 'different', 'odd', 'strange' or a 'social misfit'. Prevailing gender stereotypes might contribute to these feelings. Rudy Simone (2010), an autistic writer, points out that these societal expectations for women (such as the expectation to be 'social creatures' who cannot even go to the bathroom alone), reinforced by the media and myths of popular culture, make life even more difficult for autistic girls who might prefer to spend time alone. Kearns Miller (2003) also suggests that as women are usually considered the 'socially adept' gender, it can put a heavy burden on autistic females and might contribute to them being perceived or feeling even more 'defective', because they don't have these traditional 'female strengths'.

Some autistic women commented that they experienced some gender-based expectations from schools and school staff. Some felt that they were expected to like or dislike certain subjects or activities just because of their gender. Others felt that gender-based expectations meant that their potential was not seen.

> Teachers can have different expectations based upon students' gender. The moment my mum suggested my English teachers treat my work the same as the boys, they were much more positive because unrealistic handwriting expectations were swept aside to focus on the content of the work. (Autistic female 22)

> I hated Disney films and many other things the other girls liked or were supposed to like, so I was always on a different wavelength and never quite understood their pretend games. (Tori)

> ## Gender identity and gender dysphoria
>
> **Gender identity**
>
> Gender identity is a person's internal sense of their own identity. A person who identifies with the sex they were assigned at birth is called 'cisgender' or 'cis'. Those who do not identify with the sex they were assigned at birth may use terms such as non-binary, transgender or gender-fluid.
>
> **Gender dysphoria**
>
> Gender dysphoria is the term given to the distress or discomfort caused by the feeling of a mismatch between their physical sex and their gender identity.

There has been some evidence to suggest that there is an association between autism and gender dysphoria, with more autistic people experiencing gender dysphoria than non-autistic people, but other evidence suggests that the link is not so clear (NAS, 2023).

Many people cite social reasons as a likely reason for this possible association. Some say, for example, that autistic people are less likely to be bound by social norms, and therefore, more likely to express their authentic selves. Some studies suggest that the traits often classified as autistic could more accurately be related to the distress and discomfort caused by gender dysphoria (Fortunato et al., 2022). It is an area in which there are no definitive conclusions and it's currently a topic of much debate and research. Autistic author Abigail Balfe ('A Different Sort of Normal', 2022, p. 180) explains her feelings towards conventional binary 'rules': 'There has always been something that has felt a bit strange about the fact that I am a "girl". I looked at other girls at school and did not feel like I was "that" sort of girl. But I did not feel like ones of the boys either.'

> I spent a lot of time as a teenager questioning my gender and sexual identity. There wasn't as much information for young people twenty years ago and I didn't have the words to articulate what I was feeling. I didn't fit in with the other girls so it made me wonder what was wrong. Could I be a lesbian? Should I have been a boy? But boys were icky, always messing about and reeked of body odour or, even worse, too much yucky deodorant. No, I definitely didn't want to be a boy either. (Matilda)

Sexuality

Some studies suggest that sexuality is also more varied amongst autistic individuals, than amongst non-autistic individuals. One study (George & Stokes, 2018) suggested that 70% of autistic individuals identified with being non-heterosexual, compared with 30% of non-autistic individuals.

For many years, there has been an autism stereotype that autistic people aren't interested in sex or relationships, but this isn't the case. The autistic community does include individuals who are aromantic or asexual (those who have little or no interest in romantic or sexual relationships) as does the non-autistic community, but also includes a wide range of sexual and romantic orientations. Some research suggests that autistic people have a greater flexibility in both gender and sexual orientations, with many identifying with identities including lesbian, gay, bisexual, queer, questioning, asexual, pansexual or demisexual.

Regardless of gender or sexual identity, there can be difficulties for autistic individuals in relationships, particularly before the self-awareness that comes with diagnosis. These difficulties can relate to sensory sensitivities, communication difficulties and social difficulties, and added with low self-esteem can lead to vulnerabilities in relationships.

> I despaired that I'd never have a boyfriend. I disliked anybody hugging or touching me or even coming within a couple of metres of me. How would it ever be possible for me to get close to anybody. I wanted a boyfriend because that seemed normal, it was what my friends wanted. I was meant to want that. But I really didn't want one either. (Autistic female 11)

> Puberty was difficult, sex ed was and is designed for NTs and needs to be more accessible and inclusive of ND people. (Autistic female 1)

> I was very naïve for my age and had never been interested in having a boyfriend like the other girls. I hadn't a clue what the teachers were going on about in SRE (Sex and Relationships Education) but everybody else seemed to already know everything. I found it totally embarrassing. (Autistic female 12)

Ideas for schools

Some autistic girls might need additional support around some aspects of puberty, for example with dealing with the sensory aspect of menstruation and menstrual products and to cope with the physical changes happening in their bodies. See 'Further Reading and Resources' for some useful resources which can help with this.

Autistic girls might also benefit from additional support with Relationships and Sex Education (RSE). Low self-esteem and pressure to 'fit in' might lead to vulnerability in relationships, for example. Very clear teaching around what might constitute an unequal, harmful or coercive relationship, consent and abuse might be necessary.

> Some neurodivergent students might prefer very explicit teaching with topics around sex, as vagueness, euphemisms and metaphors might be unhelpful and a barrier to understanding (Dring-Turner, 2020)
>
> Differences in how autistic students learn and process information will be equally relevant in RSE. Some might prefer written information which they can take away, process in their own time and retain for the future. Some schools bring in outside organisations or visiting specialists to teach parts of the RSE curriculum – ensure all visitors are aware of how best to adapt their sessions to be inclusive of neurodivergent students in the group.
>
> Some might also benefit from support to explore their gender and sexual identities. Ensure mental health professionals supporting autistic students have a good understanding of autism, especially how it can present in females.

Interpreting the world

For autistic females, the world is a highly confusing and unpredictable place. Imagine the situation: You have learned all the rules; you are doing all the same things as your peers, and yet you still seem to be on a completely different wavelength, still don't seem to be able to achieve what everybody does, despite working harder than anybody you know. Your feelings and opinions seem to be dismissed by others and you're often told you're wrong, you've misunderstood, your views are unimportant. Everybody else seems to connect instinctively and so easily, whereas you always seem to inadvertently say the wrong thing. Other people say one thing but then do another. Are they deliberately being confusing and unpredictable? Sensory inputs don't seem to affect other people the way they do you. You constant feel uncomfortable. Other people seem to experience things differently than you do. You feel different, unsure of yourself and anxious all the time. Your brain works differently, on a different operating system to the majority. You interpret the world differently.

> I see the world through a web that I've cast out in order to systematise how to navigate in the world through lots and lots of different connections. The world is rich and saturated with meaning and emotions and the senses I feel like a sponge. (Samantha)

> Honesty is the best policy, right? Wrong. Well, not completely wrong. God, how confusing to anyone, let alone an ASD pupil! Apparently, it was wrong to tell a teacher – 'Miss, this is a waste of time. It's boring.' or 'Miss, you've spelt that wrong on the board. It's actually spelt ...' or even 'No, it's not that; it's actually ...'. No. No, you could never correct a teacher, even if you were being honest. But, if someone was bullying you or had stolen something from your bag or you'd made a mess, then yes, you had to be honest and tell the teacher. I was honest because the adults had told me to – that was a rule, right? And you had to follow rules. (Georgia)

Schools are usually full of rules, both official and unwritten. Many autistic students find school rules confusing and a source of much irritation and frustration, especially if applied inconsistently. 'Everyone at school lies, but when I tell them they are lying, I am the one who gets into trouble. It's not fair,' explains Laura James in her autobiography Odd Girl Out (2017, p. 48). Autistic individuals often have a strong moral code and sense of justice and may get upset when rules are ignored (Winter & Lawrence, 2011).

> I couldn't understand why rules were broken. If the teacher said that work had to be handed in on a certain date but then some people didn't hand it in, it didn't make sense. Why should I do it if others didn't? Why did they get extensions instead of punishments? (Matilda)

> Rules had to make sense. (Autistic female 11)

> Our meltdowns and angry outbursts are often due to being misunderstood and witnessing any kind of injustice. (Autistic female 12)

Some autistic students feel that rules can be oppressive and just yet another way of trying to make individuals fit in to more 'typical' ways of being.

> Frustration and sensory issues led to panic attacks. I was very quiet in primary school, but as I got older I started to talk back to teachers when rules didn't make sense or when I felt persecuted. I struggled with the idea of authority a lot and couldn't stand to stay in school, I felt oppressed and frightened. (Autistic female 14)

> Behave like this or we'll punish you, seemed to be the teachers' attitudes. Nothing ever made sense. Why should I? Why could they tell me what to do? It all made no difference. It didn't change how I felt or what I thought about things. In fact, it just made me angrier and more convinced than ever that teachers were rather a stupid breed. (Tori)

'Rewards and sanctions' policies are often in place in schools for following, or ignoring, the rules. For some autistic students, who interpret the world differently than their peers, however, the usual 'rewards' may seem pointless and might even have the opposite effect to that intended.

> For me school was for learning. I couldn't understand why this wasn't always the priority. What were 'rewards' for most other pupils (e.g., extra free time, no homework, group work), were punishments for me. (Autistic female 11)

> The kids in detention got to stay inside during lunchtime as a punishment. I hated going on the playground and would much rather have been forced to stay inside and read! Didn't seem like much of a punishment! (LJ)

I didn't want certificates or stickers or reward charts or praise. They didn't help me to fit in, and that was all I wanted. (Autistic female 22)

I followed the rules and did the work but was then called a swot. (Autistic female 10)

Is there a way to help others understand the world from an autistic perspective?

I feel like there should be a class for someone to experience one day as a person with Asperger's, having the thoughts that go a million miles per hour, the sensory issues, the indecisiveness in social situations, the awareness of being aware of being different, the bullying to an extent, the feeling of being completely alone in a room full of people, the self-doubt in relationships.

I think it's much harder for a neurotypical to understand the world from an Asperger's point of view than the other way around. Yet, we are supposed to be the ones who lack theory of mind! (Autistic female 11)

I've best heard it described like you're playing a video game. Neurotypical people are playing on an automatic setting: communication, body regulation, maintaining routine and life, all automatically. But autistic people are doing everything manually: every tiny little detail of life having to be done with conscious effort. It takes a lot of energy and it can be frustrating to handle someone with autism but I can guarantee it is more frustrating for the people experiencing life this way. (May)

Ideas for schools

Ensure rules are clear. Many autistic students need to know why rules exist. If there isn't a justifiable reason, consider scrapping the rule! Autistic students can also be particularly frustrated if rules aren't applied consistently, so make sure that all staff are using the same systems.

Clear routines and a structured day can be helpful for autistic students, and most other students. Autistic students might benefit from being told in advance about changes that are happening (e.g. substitute teachers, having to use a different classroom, fire drills).

Bear in mind that some autistic students might not respond in the usual way to rewards and sanctions. A sanction for others (e.g. staying inside at break time) might feel like a reward to an autistic student.

Use 'co-production' when designing new school environments, rules, policies and routines. Ask for, and use, the opinions of neurodivergent students and staff. Including people with lived experience in these processes will help to create more inclusive spaces, places and systems.

Advice and ideas

What sort of advice would autistic females give to younger autistic students?

> When I was a child, for the longest time, I've tried to hide my Asperger's. I tried fitting in with people who were often cruel to me because I was different, and by the time I realised I shouldn't have even attempted to try and fit into a crowd of neurotypical people, it was too late. As for the advice that can be passed down to younger female Aspies, the best advice to be given is to find out who they are before it's too late. We tend to be gifted in some areas, so instead of spending time trying to fit in with the NT crowd, spend time perfecting the gift you've been given; spend time doing the hobbies you enjoy. (Autistc female 34)

> Read about executive functioning; learn ways which work for you – lists, timers, Post-It notes. Learn about your condition, from autistic people themselves. Find which aspects affect you and how best you can work with your difficulties and when you need the world to adapt and when you need to adapt. (LJ)

> I'd learn more about myself and learn to understand why I felt the way I did. I'd learn how to manage and cope, learn about psychology, executive functioning and about introverts. I'd learn how to find what I was good at. (Autistic female 9)

> Try and develop your special interests. I write a blog – I find writing incredibly cathartic. (Autistic female 19)

> If you can find people with similar interests and skills, they may make great friends; you may make great friends at school, or you may find them later, or you may be fine without them. (LJ)

> Try to learn ways to express your feelings, be it verbally, through writing or art or music; maybe there will be someone who can help you with this. (Autistic female 12)

> Ask questions; ask for more time to study something if needed; ask for help if you need help. A fellow pupil may be able to explain something well that you don't understand, and you may be able to help another pupil in the same way. (Autistic female 21)

> Right, 15-year-old self: Don't spend so many hundreds of hours worrying, despairing and crying about being different! Instead develop more confidence to go out and do the things that are important to you. Next get yourself lots of individualised career advice to help you discover what suits you best. Don't listen to those who just tell you to be more 'normal': you'll later learn that this only really reflects their own insecurities and narrow-mindedness. Get to know, and like, yourself – the awareness and understanding of who you are is vital to your future wellbeing and success. Celebrate your differences! Oh, and another thing: You know some of those girls who you think are just being nice to you? They turn into some really meaningful and

wonderful friendships in your twenties and thirties when you are finally able to connect with and value others in your own Aspie way! Oh, and just one other thing: As hard as it may be to believe now, eventually you do become very happy just being you. (Matilda)

I'd say that I'm much happier as an adult than I ever was as a child. It gets better when you're an adult as you have more of a chance to befriend people you really like and avoid the ones you don't. Also, as you get older, you care less about what people think about you. (Autistic female 7)

When I was a child my mum used to say I'd grow out of it, when referring to all my anxiety and issues. Deep down I was terrified I'd always be this way and end up alone. When I reached college I found a group of people who accepted me fully. The bits I didn't realise yet that were autistic; how they had to find someone to look after me when they had classes because I couldn't be in the canteen alone; how they had to make decisions for me or console me for things that seemed daft and random. They did it all without question and when I found out I was autistic they were the best support system I could've asked for. Now I'm 23 and have a long-term partner and a self-made family who loves and supports who I am. I wish I could go back and tell myself that yes, you will always be this way but you will be loved for who you are, not only by the friends and family you make but also by yourself. (May)

Be yourself: be proud of who you are; work hard at what you enjoy and try your best at things you're not so good at. Don't feel bad if you can't achieve perfection. (Autistic female 6)

And what about advice for educational staff?

I went through school (and most of my adult life) undiagnosed. I was the geeky girl who blended into the background. My advice — look for those girls who seem to struggle with friendship for no apparent reason, the girls who really do well at some things but really struggle with others even when similar to the things she is good at. These are the ones who slip under the diagnosis net and don't get the help and support they need. Don't force them to work with anyone who doesn't like them, and accept they need space away from others even when they seem to be coping well. It's all an act to survive. (Autistic female 39)

I wish my teachers and peers had known I was autistic and struggling with social interactions, that my behaviour was not deliberate but just an attempt to fit in like they did. (Autistic female 6)

I wish my teachers had known how many times they and classmates had made me cry — don't assume the fairly quiet and intelligent one is happy. And don't snap. (Autistic female 8)

Lily-mai finds it comforting if she has a go-to person that she can ask for help when asked to do tasks at school. Her school actually has strategies in place. They support SEN students really well by having 1:1 s and quiet rooms if needed. (Parent of Lily-mai)

Make instructions clear and have routines. Adjust lighting, allow fidgeting (if it is not a distraction to them and others). Provide safe havens, classes, clubs and welcoming spaces to play games. People's brains work differently. Don't treat others like an idiot because they didn't understand something you found easy. There are things I find easy that others struggle with. People have strengths and weaknesses. Make the classroom a safe space where putdowns are not allowed. (Autistic female 1)

It would be good to have dogs at school. I'd like to take my dog Maisie to school! (Annie, Y7)

Have patience; ask your pupils what calms them, what worries them, what environment they work best in, what they want to learn and how. (Autistic female 12)

Learn about the condition, most notably from those with autism: Things are often described from the onlooker's point of view and assumptions made, but it can feel very different on the inside. I particularly find the term 'selectively mute' frustrating; sometimes I actually physically cannot talk; I am not choosing not to talk.

Have activities available at break times and lunch but also a quiet room if alone time is needed. Try to understand about how executive functioning difficulties affect us. (LJ)

Educational staff could learn more about autism in girls, by doing training run by autistic women. (Sue)

Most teachers have little understanding of neurodivergence. Schools are often not good spaces for ND students. Be it sensory issues with the environment and uniform or being forced to be around other people who treat them badly. (Autistic female 1)

Educational staff should be taught the different presentations of autism and how to identify them in a classroom setting. I believe the late diagnosis of autistic girls to be the biggest failure of our current educational system. The teacher training into both autism and mental health challenges should be more in-depth and thorough. Moreover, the attitude towards those with additional needs should be addressed. I've encountered many teachers who neglect or even bully certain students assuming their behaviour is due to personality flaws rather than deeper psychological reasons. Rather than accommodating autistic students or seeking alternative teaching methods, the schools I've attended seem to prefer them to work and cope independently even if this is detrimental long term. Schools as well as broader society need to adjust their expectations of autistic students. The end goal shouldn't be for us to approach things neurotypically or demand the least support from others. Such goals don't respect our natural brain development and instead negate responsibility from educational staff onto the child themselves. Additionally, for autistic students who succeeded academically – like me – there is a complete lack of understanding that the same competence may not be said of other aspects of school life. My above-average grades were repeatedly used against me as proof that I should be able to cope without accommodations. This attitude comes back to the general lack of understanding about autism amongst educational staff. The obsessive focus on academic success inhibits staff from seeing students as whole people that may still benefit from wellbeing interventions regardless of their high grades. Those who achieved the highest GCSE and A-level results at my high school were often at the same time desperately struggling with poor physical and mental health. (Alis)

Supporting families

The focus of this book has been to investigate the school and college experiences of autistic girls. However, it is important to remember that there will also be difficulties and differences in the home environment too, as well as in other aspects of daily life such as socialising, leisure activities and accessing health and care services.

Some autistic girls might have more obvious difficulties in one environment than another. For example, it is not uncommon for some to be 'model pupils' at school, working hard, following the rules and seemingly coping, only to arrive home and let out all the frustrations and anxieties that have built up during the school day, resulting in shutdowns, meltdowns or a need to withdraw. Other students might not demonstrate such obvious difficulties when at home in comfortable surroundings with people who understand them, but might experience more obvious difficulties when in the school and other environments where the sensory, social, learning and communication expectations are much greater. These differences and discrepancies can sometimes add to the delay in diagnosis of autistic girls, as difficulties might not be immediately apparent in the school environment. It can also be a source of much frustration to parents and carers who might feel that the school does not 'see' their child's difficulties or does not believe the difficulties they are experiencing at home.

Parents and carers are often affected by having an autistic child. For example, they might:

- Spend a lot of time advocating for their child and attending assessments and meetings, which can be exhausting as well as time-consuming, and feel frustrated at having to repeat information to many different professionals.

- Not know how best to support their child at home, especially before a diagnosis is confirmed.

- Not feel that their child gets the support they need, either at school or for mental health conditions.

- Feel their concerns aren't taken seriously or are dismissed by education and health professionals who are not aware of different presentations of autism, or who don't see their child's difficulties in certain settings. They might feel they are being labelled as 'anxious' or 'over-protective' by professionals for voicing their concerns.

- Experience negative reactions, denial or disbelief from family members or the community about their child's diagnosis.
- Spend months or years waiting for assessments and a formal diagnosis.
- Feel isolated or socially excluded.
- Experience practical difficulties such as the practicalities of caring for a child who cannot attend school or difficulties accessing specialist equipment or support.
- Be going through their own journey of self-discovery. A child receiving a diagnosis of autism can lead to some parents realising that they themselves, or other family members, are also autistic.

Ideas for schools

Signpost families to useful sources of support – this might include reliable websites/organisations, local services and support groups for autistic young people or their families.

Hold support group or information sessions at your establishment in order to share ideas and information about autism.

Take parents' and carers' concerns seriously and ensure they feel listened to. Be clear about the next steps in the assessment process and what they can expect from the school. Make parents aware that a formal diagnosis will not change their child, and does not necessarily lead automatically to additional support. Ensure parents are clear about the support available to them and their child while waiting for a diagnosis.

Share information regularly as a two-way process. Make it easy for parents to contact a named key worker at the school and share strategies that are successful at home.

Final thoughts

This chapter has brought together experiences of school and education from autistic females. Of course, there is lots more to say about autism – how it affects females at home, in family life, in relationships, in the workplace and when accessing health and social care, for example. The 'Further Reading and Resources' section at the end of this book can signpost you to some resources if you are interested in finding out more.

But by now, you'll be beginning to understand what an autistic girl's experience of education can be like. You've seen how hard it is for many of them. Just the physical school environment can be a bombardment of the senses, causing discomfort, pain, meltdowns and shutdowns. Then on top of that the difficulties with friendships, with communication, with social times. The difficulties with transitions, coping with change, with interpreting others' behaviours. The difficulties that are associated with low self-esteem and the constant anxiety many experience. The total exhaustion that comes from masking, from trying to fit in, from having to function in a world not designed for your needs, from trying to hide all of these difficulties. The frustration that comes with being academically able but somehow unable to show this in the ways the curriculum demands.

What's noticeable is how invisible so many of these difficulties are. To the observer, so many of these girls are 'coping', 'managing' or even 'doing well' because they are quiet, achieving good grades and well-behaved. I hope that this chapter has shined a light on the invisible difficulties related to autism, and on the importance of recognising these difficulties. It's worth repeating that this doesn't only apply to girls, there are many autistic boys who fit this profile of autism too, and, of course, some girls whose autism presents in the more 'traditional' way.

I hope this chapter has highlighted that autistic individuals have strengths, skills, talents, feelings and needs just as every other individual and that the autistic way of being is not inferior to any other way, simply different. I also want to draw attention to the fact that autism itself is often not what causes problems in the school environment; more often it is the lack of understanding from others and the assumption and expectation that everybody acts, feels, thinks and interprets information in the same way.

There are plenty of changes that can be made in educational settings that can support inclusion of autistic students. Many of these are easy and inexpensive to implement but can make a big difference. Most simply require a change of attitude and change of perspective – the recognition that the current school system has not been designed for neurodivergent students who think, learn and interpret the world differently.

> Although people are a confusing puzzle I swear I'll never understand and my senses are so alert it hurts sometimes, there's some really wonderful things about being autistic. I notice things other people don't, see ways out of situations others can't, and seem to almost always find the motivation and…well, I'm just me and that can be super cool. (Autistic female 3)

References

ADDitude (2022) *PMDD, Autism and ADHD: The Hushed Comorbidity.* Available from: additudemag.com/pmdd-autism-adhd/ [accessed on 18 January 2023].

Atkinson M. & Hornby G., (2002) *Mental Health Handbook for Schools.* London: RoutledgeFalmer.

Attwood T. (2007) *The Complete Guide To Asperger's Syndrome.* London: Jessica Kingsley Publishers.

Autistica (2022) *Alexithymia.* Available from: autistica.org.uk/what-is-autism/anxiety-and-autism-hub/alexithymia [accessed 5 December 2022].

Baldwin S. & Costley D. (2015) The experiences and needs of females with high-functioning autism spectrum disorders. *Autism,* 6/2015, 1–13.

Balfe A. (2021) *A Different Sort of Normal.* London: Puffin Books.

Begley J. (2014) Connect: the development of an online social network for people on the autism spectrum and their families. *Good Autism Practice,* 15, 2, 15.

Book Trust (2013) *Book Trust Reading Habits Survey 2013.* Available from: www.booktrust.org.uk/usr/library/documents/main/1576-booktrust-reading-habits-report-final.pdf

Bristol Autism Support (2022) *Autism and Executive Functioning.* Available from: bristolautismsupport.org/autism-and-executive-functioning/ [accessed on 22 November 2022].

Cuijpers P. (1997) Bibliotherapy in unipolar depression: a meta-analysis. *Journal of Behaviour Therapy and Experimental Psychiatry,* 28 (2), 139–147.

Den Boer P.C., Wiersma D. & Van den Bossch R.J. (2004) Why is self-help neglected in the treatment of emotional disorder? A meta-analysis. *Psychological Medicine,* 34(6), 959–971.

Dring-Turner H. (2020) *Recognition, representation, and relationships: how the UK Relationships and Sex Education Curriculum (2020) can meet the needs of and offer representation to young disabled and neurodivergent or neurodiverse people with LGBT+ identities. A thesis submitted in partial fulfilment of the requirements for the degree of Doctor of Philosophy.* Department of Educational Research: Lancaster University, UK. Available from: eprints.lancs.ac.uk/id/eprint/179534/1/2022Dring_TurnerPhD.pdf [accessed 3 February 2023].

Fanner D. & Urquart C. (2008) Bibliotherapy for mental health service users: a systematic review. *Health Information and Libraries Journal,* 5, (4), December 2008, 237–252.

Finkenauer C., Pollmann M., Begeer S. & Kerkof P. (2012) Brief Report: Examining the link between autistic traits and compulsive internet use in a non-clinical sample. *Journal of Autism Development Disorders,* 42, 10, 2252–2256.

Fortunato A., Giovanardi G., Innocenzi E., Mirabella M., Caviglia G., Lingiardi V. & Speranza A.M. (2022) Is it autism? A critical commentary on the co-occurrence of gender dysphoria and autism spectrum disorder. *J. Homosex.* 69(7):1204–1221. doi: 10.1080/00918369.2021.1905385. Epub 2021 Apr 14. PMID: 33852376.

Gadsby, H. (2022) *Hannah Gadsby on her autism diagnosis: 'I've always been plagued by a sense I was a little out of whack'.* The Guardian Online 19 March 2022. Available from: theguardian.com/stage/2022/mar/19/hannah-gadsby-autism-diagnosis-little-out-of-whack [accessed on 18 January 2023].

Gibbs, S. (2021) *Drama Queen: One Autistic Woman and a Life of Unhelpful Labels.* London: Hachette.

George R. & Stokes M.A. (2018) Sexual orientation in autism spectrum disorder. *Autism Res.* 1(1):133–141. doi: 10.1002/aur.1892. Epub 2017 Nov 21. PMID: 29159906.

Gould J. & Ashton-Smith J. (2011) Missed diagnosis or misdiagnosis? Girls and women on the autism spectrum. *Good Autism Practice Journal*, 12: 34–41.

Holliday Willey L. (1999) *Pretending to be Normal.* London: Jessica Kingsley Publishers.

Hull L., Petrides K.V., Allison C., Smith P., Baron-Cohen S., Lai, M.C. & Mandy, W. (2017) 'Putting on my best normal': Social camouflaging in adults with autism spectrum conditions. *Journal of Autism and Developmental Disorders*, 47(8): 2519–2534. https://doi.org/0.1007/ s10803-017-3166-5

James L. (2017) *Odd Girl Out.* London: Pan McMillan.

Jamison T.R. & Schuttler J.O. (2015) Examining social competence, self-perception, quality of life and internalizing and externalizing symptoms in adolescent females with and without autism spectrum disorders: a quantitative design including between-groups and correlational analyses. *Molecular Autism*, 17, 6–53.

Joyce C. et al. (2017) Anxiety, intolerance of uncertainty and restricted and repetitive behaviour: Insights directly from young people with ASD. *Journal of Autism and Developmental Disorders*, 47(2): 3789–3802.

Kearns Miller J. (2003) *Women from Another Planet. Our Lives in the Universe of Autism.* Bloomington, IN: First Books.

Kidd D. & Castano E. (2013) Reading literary fiction improves theory of mind. *Science*, 342 (6156): 377–380.

Kranjc J. (2011) *Ace Project*, Autism Connections Europe. Center for Autism Slovenia. Presentation slides London, 24 November 2011.

Lugnegård T., Hallerbäck M.U. & Gillberg C. (2011) Psychiatric comorbidity in young adults with a clinical diagnosis of Asperger syndrome. *Research in Developmental Disabilities*, 32(5): 1910–1917.

McGhee K., Morris S. & Pahil R. (2011) *Speech and Language Difficulties: Module Code 1105515 Unit 4: Adolescent Development.* Birmingham, UK: University of Birmingham.

McGirl P. (2009) *Mental Health Skills for Schools Handbook.* Worcestershire County Council: Worcestershire Targeted Mental Health in Schools Project.

McNicholl, E. (2023) *Writing on the National Autistic Society Website: 'Stories from the Spectrum: Elle McNicoll'.* Available from: autism.org.uk/advice-and-guidance/stories/stories-from-the-spectrum-elle-mcnicoll [accessed on 18 January 2023].

NAS – National Autistic Society (2023) *Autism and Gender Identity.* Available from: autism.org.uk/advice-and-guidance/what-is-autism/autism-and-gender-identity [accessed 5 January 2023].

Obaydi H. & Puri B.K. (2008) Prevalence of premenstrual syndrome in autism: a prospective observer-rated study. *The Journal of International Medical Research*, 36(2), 268–272. https://doi.org/10.1177/147323000803600208

Poe, C. A. (2019) *How to be Autistic.* London: Myriad Editions.

Rodgers J., Wigham S., McConachie H., Freeston M., Honey E. & Parr J.R. (2016) Development of the Anxiety Scale for Children with autism spectrum disorder (ASC-ASD). *Autism Research*, 9(11): 1205–1215.

Shane-Simpson C., et al. (2016) Associations between compulsive internet use and autism spectrum. *Research in Autism Spectrum Disorders*, 23: 152–165.

Simone R. (2010) *Aspergirls.* Jessica Kingsley Publishers: London.

SMIRA – Selective Mutism Information and Research Association (2023) *About Selective Mutism.* Available at www.selectivemutism.org.uk/about-selective-mutism/ [accessed 5 January 2023].

Thunberg, G. (2019) *CBS News 'Teen activist Greta Thunberg on how Asperger's helps her fight climate change'.* Available from: cbsnews.com/news/greta-thunberg-climate-change-gift-of-aspergers/ [accessed 17 January 2023].

Van Steensel F.J., Bogels S.M. & Perrin S. (2011) Anxiety disorders in children and adolescents with autistic spectrum disorders: A meta-analysis. *Clinical Child and Family Psychology Review*, 14(3): 302–317.

Wigham S. et al. (2015) The interplay between sensory processing abnormalities, intolerance of uncertainty, anxiety and restricted and repetitive behaviours in autism spectrum disorder. *Journal of Autism and Developmental Disorders*, 45(4): 943–952.

Winter M. & Lawrence C. (2011) *Asperger Syndrome: What Teachers Need to Know*, second edition. London: Jessica Kingsley Publishers.

Part 4
Practical resources

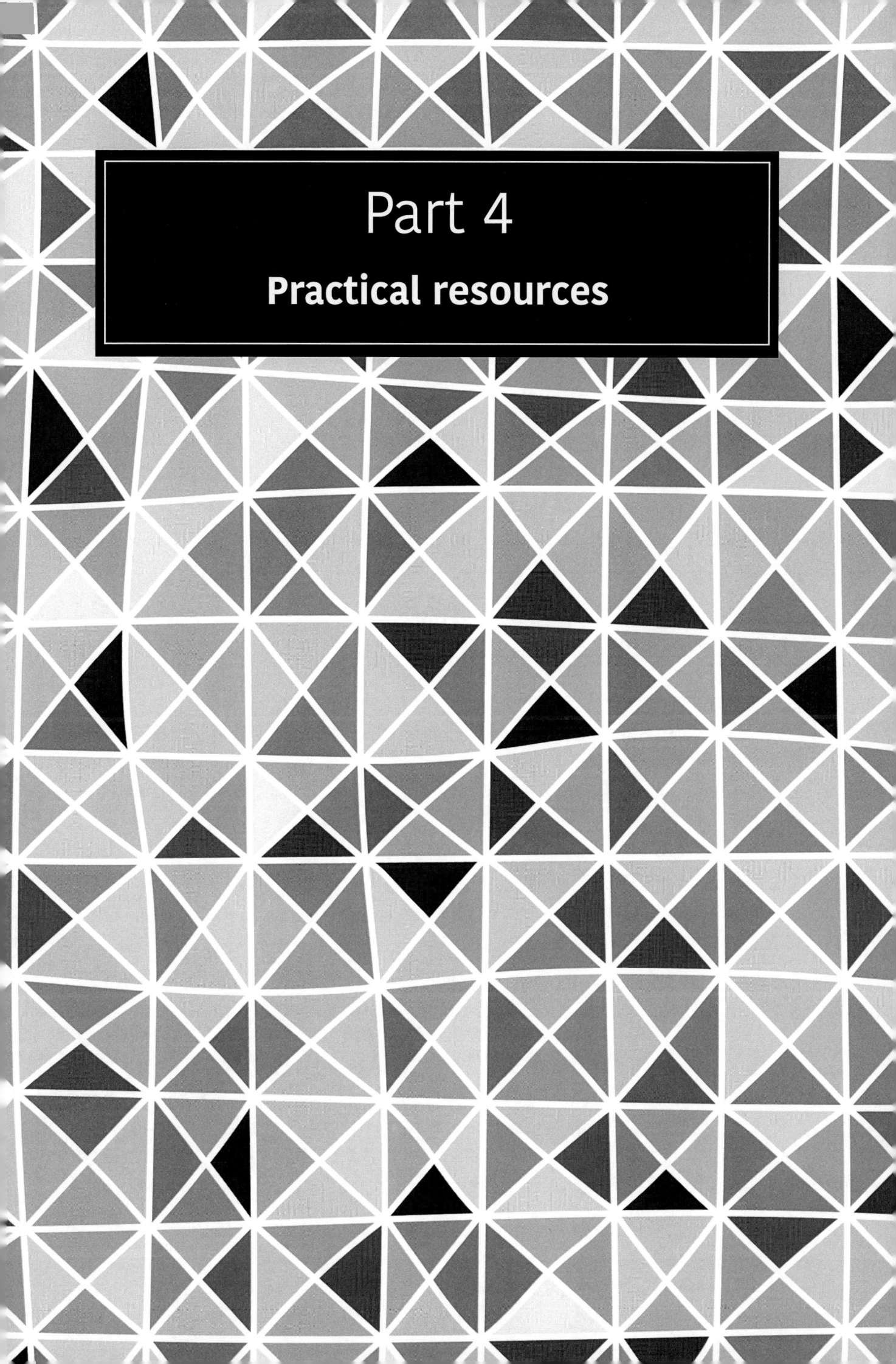

PART 4: PRACTICAL RESOURCES

School, staff and environmental audits

As you've learned from the previous chapter, the physical school environment, school policies and rules and a lack of understanding of autism can create difficulties for autistic students. These resources begin with audits for the school that can help to create more inclusive environments, along with information sheets that can be shared with staff. Most of these resources are designed to support schools in supporting all neurodivergent students, not just autistic students. Sometimes it can be overwhelming for school staff to believe they need to be doing one set of things for autistic students, another set for ADHD students, another set for dyslexic students and so on. Of course, individuals in these groups all have different needs and should not be considered a homogeneous group, but there are also lots of strategies that can help many of these students (and many other students too).

1. School self-audit

For: School leadership teams and Special/Additional Needs Co-ordinators

Instructions: Rate yourself for each area. Use this to identify your priorities to work on as a setting (and congratulate yourself on what you do well!).

	We don't do this yet	This could be improved	We're making progress with this	We do this well
All teaching staff have had training on neurodiversity in the classroom, including training on autism and autistic girls				
All non-teaching staff (e.g. dinner time staff, administrators, mentors) have had training on neurodiversity				
We use co-production, working with neurodivergent staff and students before implementing new policies, practices, rules and environments				
Our physical environment is accessible and appropriate for neurodivergent individuals (see separate audit)				
All visiting teachers, substitute teachers and student teachers are provided with information about neurodivergent students and their individual needs				
Staff use strategies to communicate for neurodiversity (see separate audit)				
We have checked our school rules and policies do not discriminate against neurodivergent, disabled or other minority-group students				

PART 4: PRACTICAL RESOURCES

	We don't do this yet	This could be improved	We're making progress with this	We do this well
We work closely with families of neurodivergent students and use their expertise to support individual students				
Students can access support in a variety of ways (e.g. through e-mail or written means as well as approaching staff face-to-face)				
Our school library/reading areas contain books with neurodivergent protagonists, written by neurodivergent authors				
We provide/can refer to specialist support for neurodivergent students, such as counsellors, mentors and peer-support groups				
Quiet spaces are provided for students who need to use them, both at social times and for learning				
A range of activities is provided at social times for students who find the playground difficult				
Students know how to report bullying and that this is dealt with promptly				
Actions to take:				

2. Neurodiverse-friendly environment audits

(a) School/educational establishment audit

For: School leaders and SENCOs

Instructions: Rate the whole school environment (see separate audit for individual classrooms). Identify areas to improve and the actions that need to be taken.

	Needs improving	**Okay**	**We do this well**
Corridors are easy to navigate. One-way systems or staggered class exit times are in place to avoid crowding in narrow corridors			
Corridors are kept clutter-free			
Spaces are provided on the playground for students who prefer alternative/quieter/individual activities (e.g. a reading corner, a games table)			
Quiet spaces are provided for any students who need down-time at social times (e.g. a quiet room or library)			
Quiet spaces are kept quiet, naturally lit and clutter-free			
The dining hall/canteen is managed to reduce crowds of students			
There are quiet spaces available for students to eat			
Assemblies and other large gatherings are managed to be accessible for students who need greater personal space than others			
Classrooms, buildings and other rooms are labelled clearly with words and symbols/pictures			
Consistency of signage is used around the setting (e.g. clear symbols and signs to indicate where students are allowed and what they can/can't do)			
Actions to take:			

(b) Other settings environmental audit

For: Health or education professionals working in non-school environments

Instructions: Rate your physical environment. Identify areas for improvement and actions to take.

	Needs improving	**Okay**	**We do this well**
The building is easy to navigate with clear signage			
Rooms and spaces are clearly labelled			
Consistency of signage is used around the setting (e.g. clear symbols and signs)			
All staff (e.g. receptionists, assistants, trainees) are aware of the needs of neurodivergent individuals and how to communicate most effectively			
Waiting areas are kept: • Naturally lit • Clutter free • Quiet • Uncrowded			
Quiet spaces are provided – and kept quiet – for any service user who needs somewhere quiet to wait or rest			
Rooms for activities, therapies and meetings are: • Naturally lit • Clutter free • Free from background noise • Sufficient in size for personal space needs			
Actions to take:			

(c) Classroom neurodivergent-friendly environmental audit

For: Classroom teachers of all ages/subjects

Instructions: Rate your individual classroom. Identify areas to improve and actions you could take.

	Needs improving	Okay	We do this well
The classroom is naturally lit when possible. Bright and fluorescent lighting is avoided			
Background noise is eliminated or reduced as much as possible (e.g. noise from outside and neighbouring classrooms, noise from equipment/heating/air conditioning/projectors)			
The classroom is kept clutter-free, especially desks, tables and surfaces			
Equipment and resources have a designated place to be stored. They are labelled clearly with words, symbols and/or pictures for ease of access for students			
Desks and chairs are arranged so that students have sufficient personal space around them and can move around the classroom easily			
Wall displays are kept relevant, up-to-date and well-presented (i.e. not visually overwhelming)			
Visually overwhelming patterns and displays are avoided (e.g. zigzags and stripes can be difficult for some students)			
Areas around the screen/board are kept clear and clutter-free to aid concentration			
Tables and chairs are the correct height for students using them			
Useful equipment and resources are provided for any student who needs them – e.g. coloured overlays, support cushions, pencil grips, writing slopes, dictionaries, number lines			
Sufficient space is provided for practical tasks such as getting changed, arts and crafts, construction			
A quiet space is accessible for any student who needs to work somewhere quieter			
Actions to take:			

PART 4: PRACTICAL RESOURCES

3. Communicating for neurodiversity

(a) Communication in the classroom

For: Classroom teachers and teaching assistants

Instructions: Use this self-audit to identify how you communicate for neurodiversity in the classroom. Identify any strategies you could introduce or try out in your classroom.

Do you:	
Eliminate background noise and other distractions before talking to the class?	
Ensure you have a student's attention before speaking to them (e.g. by using their name/eliminating distractions)?	
Share the structure of the day/lesson (e.g. using a visual timetable)?	
Discuss any changes to plan or changes to routine?	
Give instructions clearly in the order they are to be carried out?	
Use visuals (e.g. a list, objects, examples, photos, pictures, diagrams) to back-up your verbal instructions and explanations?	
Explain any new vocabulary and non-literal language?	
Give clear instructions about what students are to do, rather than what not to do (e.g. 'Walk slowly' can be clearer than 'Stop running')?	
State clearly how long students have to spend on a task and how much work is required?	
Allow sufficient processing time for students to make sense of information and instructions before moving on to the next piece of information?	
Allow sufficient, unhurried processing time before expecting students to answer a question?	
Give students time to prepare or rehearse their answers if appropriate?	
Check students' understanding by asking them to show you what they have to do or to explain in their own words?	
Break down tasks into smaller steps and provide visual reminders, such as a checklist or visual list of instructions?	
Provide clear, written (or other visual) instructions for homework tasks?	
Ensure that written information (on screen or printed) is presented in an easy-to-read font, large enough and on an appropriate background (black on white is difficult for some students)?	
Ensure that written information (on screen or printed) is well-spaced and not overwhelming?	
Ensure that visual support (e.g. pictures, photos, symbols, background) for written and spoken information is clear, relevant and helpful rather than confusing?	
Manage group work appropriately by allocating the groups and having clear expectations?	

Do you:	
Know individual student's communication preferences? (e.g. knowing how to avoid unnecessary anxiety for students with selective mutism or other anxieties around communication)	
Cultivate a classroom in which it is the norm for students to seek clarification, ask for help and ask questions?	
Provide useful resources that students can access independently (e.g. key vocabulary lists, numberlines, dictionaries)?	
Strategies I'm going to try:	

PART 4: PRACTICAL RESOURCES

(b) Communication in other settings

For: Health, education and social care professionals working with neurodivergent individuals in other settings

Instructions: Use this self-audit to identify areas you could improve your communication style with neurodivergent individuals.

Do you:	
Provide sufficient information to service users in advance about the location, timings and what to expect?	
Provide alternative means of communication for individuals who might experience phone anxiety (e.g. email, text, messaging)?	
Eliminate background noise and other distractions before beginning?	
Share the structure of the session (e.g. using visuals)?	
Discuss any changes to plan or changes to routine?	
Use visuals (e.g. a list, objects, examples, photos, pictures, diagrams) to back-up your verbal instructions and explanations?	
Explain any technical vocabulary and non-literal language?	
Allow sufficient processing time for service users to make sense of information before moving on (e.g. by speaking slowly and adding in pauses)?	
Allow sufficient, unhurried processing time before expecting service users to answer a question?	
Give service users questions in advance of the meeting, if appropriate, so they have time to prepare answers.	
Check service users' understanding by asking them to explain in their own words?	
Break down larger activities into smaller, more manageable chunks, using visuals such as a checklist?	
Provide clear, written (or other visual) information about what service users are to do before subsequent sessions, or as a reminder of the topics covered in a session?	
Ensure that written information (on screen or printed) is presented in an easy-to-read font, large enough and on an appropriate background (black on white is difficult for some students)?	
Ensure that written information (on screen or printed) is well-spaced and not overwhelming?	
Ensure that visual support (e.g. pictures, photos, symbols, background) for written and spoken information is clear, relevant and helpful rather than confusing?	
Manage any group tasks appropriately by allocating the groups and having clear expectations?	

Know individual service user's communication preferences (e.g. knowing how to avoid unnecessary anxiety for individuals with selective mutism or other anxieties around communication)?	
Cultivate an environment in which it is the norm for service users to seek clarification and ask questions?	
Strategies I'm going to try:	

PART 4: PRACTICAL RESOURCES

4. Student/service user profiles

(a) Student profile

For: All staff working with a student

Instructions: Complete in conjunction with the student. Students might prefer to work with a member of staff that they know well, such as a class teacher, teaching assistant or SENCO. Share with all staff working with the student, including substitute teachers, trainee teachers and visiting staff. Ensure that profiles are updated frequently.

Student Profile	
Name:	Year Group/Class:
My strengths, skills and likes:	Things I find difficult:
Strategies that help me in class:	
Staff can help me by:	
Other information staff need to know about me:	

EDUCATING AND SUPPORTING AUTISTIC GIRLS

(b) Service user profile

For: Service users/clients in settings other than the classroom

Instructions: Service users to complete (with support from a professional if required) and share with the professionals working with them in other settings.

Individual Profile	
Name:	Age:
My communication needs:	My sensory needs:
My strengths, skills and likes:	Things I find difficult:
Other things you need to know about me:	

PART 4: PRACTICAL RESOURCES

5. Neurodiversity need-to-knows

For: All staff across a setting

Instructions: This is a brief fact sheet about neurodiversity to share with staff.

Neurodiversity: need-to-knows!

Neurodiversity is short for 'neurological diversity'. Neurodiversity simply means that there is a range of ways in which human brains function. In other words, our brains do not all process information in the same way, but rather **we think, learn, process information and relate to others in different ways**.

Neurodiversity is a totally natural and normal aspect of human variation. Unfortunately, environments, systems and practices in everyday life have generally **been designed only for the neurotypical population**.

Neurotypical (NT) – Having a style of neurocognitive functioning that falls within the current societal classification of 'normal'.

This means that neurodivergent individuals are often placed at a disadvantage. They have to try twice as hard as everybody else in order to live in **a world not designed for their way of being**.

Neurodivergent (ND) – Having a style of neurocognitive functioning which falls outside this idea of 'normal'. Individuals with diagnoses of conditions such as autism, dyslexia, dyspraxia, dyscalculia and ADHD are considered neurodivergent.

Current figures suggest that:

10% of the population are thought to be dyslexic (British Dyslexia Association, 2023a)

6% of the population are thought to be dyscalculic (BDA, 2023b)

5% of the population are thought to have ADHD (ADHD UK, 2023)

5% of the population are thought to be dyspraxic (Dyspraxia Foundation, 2023)

Over 1% of the population are thought to be autistic (National Autistic Society, 2023)

Therefore, you should expect, and accept, that a significant proportion of the student population is neurodivergent. Many neurodivergent students benefit from: changes to the physical school environment; clear communication from staff; opportunities to learn and work in their own ways; understanding and acceptance from others; and working in an accepting environment in which it is normal to be different.

6. Top ten tips for supporting neurodivergent students

For: All teachers, teaching assistants and support staff

Instructions: A 'quick tips' sheet of ten strategies that can help neurodivergent students in the classroom to share with staff.

Top Ten Tips: Supporting Neurodiversity in the Classroom

1 **Allow extra processing time.** Neurodivergent students might need longer to think about questions and their answers.

2 **Use visual support.** Back up what you are saying with visuals such as photos, objects, diagrams, flow charts, symbols or written information.

3 **Break down bigger tasks into small, manageable chunks.** Give step-by-step instructions to support students to start and work through a task.

4 **Support memory load.** Provide visual reminders of instructions and information, especially for homework or extended tasks.

5 **Remove sensory distractions.** Eliminate background noise when possible, remove unnecessary clutter, keep displays relevant and clear.

6 **Provide useful resources.** Some students might find desk slopes, wobble cushions, tinted overlays, pencil grips, dictionaries, numberlines or key vocabulary sheets useful.

7 **Present information clearly.** Use clear fonts, backgrounds and spacing. Keep visuals relevant.

8 **Allow students to work in their own ways.** Many students will know how they learn best.

9 **Get to know individual students.** No two neurodivergent students are the same. Get to know the individuals' strengths, likes and needs.

10 **Be accepting of difference.** Cultivate an atmosphere in which it is normal to be different. Normal to ask for help. Normal to find some things easier and other things harder. Normal to learn in different ways.

PART 4: PRACTICAL RESOURCES

7. Autism across subject areas

For: Teachers and teaching assistants

Instructions: A brief guide to challenges for autistic students across subject areas and how to support these differences. Can be shared with classroom teachers and subject-specific staff, as well as teaching assistants supporting autistic students.

Subject	Possible challenges for autistic students (not all students will have difficulty in all of these areas)	Support students by:
English	• 'Reading between the lines' of text and understanding hidden meanings and inference • Understanding idioms, metaphors and other non-literal language • Understanding characters' feelings and motives • Role-playing activities and 'putting themselves in the shoes of others' • Interpreting facial expression and nonverbal communication when watching drama or film • Writing fiction from another person's perspective • Planning ahead for longer essays and extended writing • Sticking to answering the question • Understanding that there might be neither 'right' nor 'wrong' answers • Interpreting questions	• Explaining hidden meanings, idioms, metaphors and non-literal language • Discussing characters' feelings and motives explicitly • Checking understanding regularly • Providing planning frames and structure for longer answers • Being clear that different answers can be equally 'right' • Giving clear instructions and questions • Stating how long answers need to be
Humanities	• 'Putting themselves in the shoes' of historical figures or people from the past • Structuring longer pieces of extended writing • Sticking to answering the question • Understanding a range of perspectives and views	• Provide planning frames and structure for longer pieces of work • Discuss historical figures' motives, beliefs and feelings

(*Continued*)

Copyright material from Victoria Honeybourne (2024), *Educating and Supporting Autistic Girls*, Routledge

117

Subject	Possible challenges for autistic students (not all students will have difficulty in all of these areas)	Support students by:
Maths	• Showing all the working out • Working through all stages of a problem	• Allow students to work in their own way if they reach the correct answers that way
Languages	• Participating in role plays • Speaking aloud in class	• Allow other ways of contributing – for example, speaking with a trusted partner or 1:1 with an adult
Art and Design	• Accepting praise and criticism • Working on joint projects • Understanding there may be more than one way to do something	• Teach giving and receiving feedback skills explicitly • Allocate partners or groups carefully • Give clear roles to each member of a group and make group work rules clear • Explain explicitly that there are different ways of completing a piece of work
Science	• May be sensory issues relating to the smells in a science laboratory • Might be physical issues relating to clumsiness, body awareness and motor skills	• Be aware of individual students' sensory needs and how this can impact on their learning • Ensure students have sufficient personal space for practical work and support when needed • Label equipment clearly and provide clear teaching on how to use equipment safely
PE	• Playing team sports with others • Difficulties with gross-motor skills and body awareness • Sensory issues relating to PE kit • Safety issues and recognising risks • Coping with communal changing rooms	• Provide a range of activities, not just team sports • Allow students to get changed privately • Allow sufficient time for students to get changed • Allocate teams or groups carefully

Subject	Possible challenges for autistic students (not all students will have difficulty in all of these areas)	Support students by:
		• Provide opportunities for students to practice skills in an unhurried, stress-free environment • Ensure sufficient personal space for students when getting changed, practicing skills and taking part • Allow students to wear PE kit they feel comfortable in (as long as it is safe) • Tell students in advance about changes to activities
Food Technology	• There may be sensory issues relating to smell, touch and texture of certain foods • Difficulties relating to motor skills, body awareness and using equipment	• Be aware of individual students' sensory and physical needs • Allow students to adapt recipes to meet their sensory needs • Ensure sufficient personal space for practical tasks and provide easy-to-use equipment
Music	• May be sensory issues relating to noise • Group work may cause difficulties • Playing in time with others may cause difficulties	• Be aware of individual students' sensory and physical needs • Allow the use of headphones when needed • Allow students to practise in quieter areas
Design Technology	• May be sensory issues relating to the noise of machines in a workshop • Motor skills may impact confidence and progress	• Be aware of individual students' sensory and physical needs • Provide extra support when needed • Ensure sufficient personal space when doing practical tasks • Provide easy-to-use tools

8. Autism: what (not) to say

For: All professionals working with autistic students

Instructions: Some people can find it difficult to know what to say to autistic students as they fear they might inadvertently upset or offend the individual, or make the situation worse. Some common responses can also cause unintentional harm sometimes. This is a guidance sheet to share with staff supporting autistic students.

Working with autistic individuals: what (not) to say

Terminology:

Language around autism and neurodiversity is changing all the time. At the current time, research suggests most autistic people prefer identity-first language (*autistic individual*) rather than person-first language (*individual with autism*), as they see their autism as an integral part of them, not something that can be separated from them. Some autism people prefer to use other terms such as 'on the autism spectrum' or 'Asperger syndrome' to describe themselves. Use the terms the autistic individual prefers.

When talking about autism, it is preferable to **avoid** using terms such as: disease; disorder; handicap; mental illness; 'suffers from'; 'an autistic'; high/low functioning; severe/mild autism.

Supporting autistic individuals:

Some common responses can sometimes cause unintentional distress to autistic individuals. Many people use these phrases without thinking. Try to notice what you use and replace with alternatives.

Avoid saying:

You don't look autistic. (This is not seen as a compliment, but often interpreted as the speaker not believing the person is autistic. Autism is an invisible difference. You won't know somebody is autistic just by looking at them.)

You must only be mildly autistic. (Functioning labels such as high/low functioning and mild/severe autism aren't considered helpful. Just because an autistic person has low support needs in a certain situation doesn't mean they have low support needs in all situations at all times.)

Everyone is a bit autistic/on the autism spectrum somewhere. (Nope. If everybody was on the autism spectrum, then there would be far more understanding and acceptance of autism!)

PART 4: PRACTICAL RESOURCES

Can't you just try a bit harder? (Autistic people are often already trying ten times harder than neurotypicals in order to fit into a world not designed for their way of being. Masking, or pretending to fit in and be something they are not, can be exhausting for autistic individuals and lead to low self-esteem and lack of self-compassion.)

Just forget about it. (Many autistic people can't just 'forget about' a problem. There can be a tendency to ruminate and over-think, especially if they don't understand why something has occurred. Many autistic people want to understand a situation, but it might seem to others that they keep bringing up something that others have moved on from.)

Self-awareness

This section of resources focuses on developing self-awareness, self-esteem and a sense of wellbeing in autistic girls. Activities are included to support autistic girls to develop a sense of who they are and to identify what is important to them as individuals. Autistic girls can lack a secure sense of self-identity (Simone, 2010). This might be due to spending a lot of time masking their true self in order to fit in with those around them. They can pick up on messages from other people, societal norms and the media that their way of being isn't as valid as neurotypicals. Having a sense of self-awareness and wellbeing can also be an essential first step for some autistic individuals before being able to understand their anxiety and being able to engage with therapies such as cognitive behavioural therapy (Spectrum Gaming, 2022).

There are no right or wrong answers to any of these activities, and each individual will develop the activities in their own way. The activities can be completed in many different ways – either written, with pictures, through discussion, using digital methods, etc. It is important that the ideas come from the individuals themselves and are not 'imposed' on them by adults supporting them. This is particularly important when working with neurodivergent individuals who interpret the world differently, sometimes having different values and priorities than neurotypicals. It is important that staff do not try to impose 'typical' values, goals or beliefs, and promote the fact that neurodivergent ways of interpreting the world are just as valid.

PART 4: PRACTICAL RESOURCES

1. Who am I?

For: Students

Instructions: Students to complete in any way they like – using words, pictures or photos for example. Can be used to start up a conversation with students to get to know them, or as an ice-breaker activity for groups.

Name:	Age:
My favourite… colour TV show animal book food school subject game	
Words that describe me:	My hobbies and interests:
I'm good at:	I find difficult:

1. Who am I?

2. Who am I? Part 2

For: Older students/service users

Instructions: For students to complete. Again, this could be used as a way to get to know new students/service users or as a basis to start discussion and support.

What I like to do for fun:	The achievement I am most proud of:	When I overcame a problem or fear:
My perfect day would be …	My best memory:	My dreams for the future:
How other people would describe me:	How I would describe myself:	Things I find confusing:
Something I would like to get better at:	Something I have learned about myself:	What makes me 'me':

PART 4: PRACTICAL RESOURCES

3. What's important to me?

For: Students

Instructions: Again, this could be used as an activity to get to know students/service users and what is important to them.

Make a spider diagram, poster or collage of the things that are important to you at the moment. You might like to think about these categories: school or college, hobbies and interests, friends, family, home, the community, wider issues.

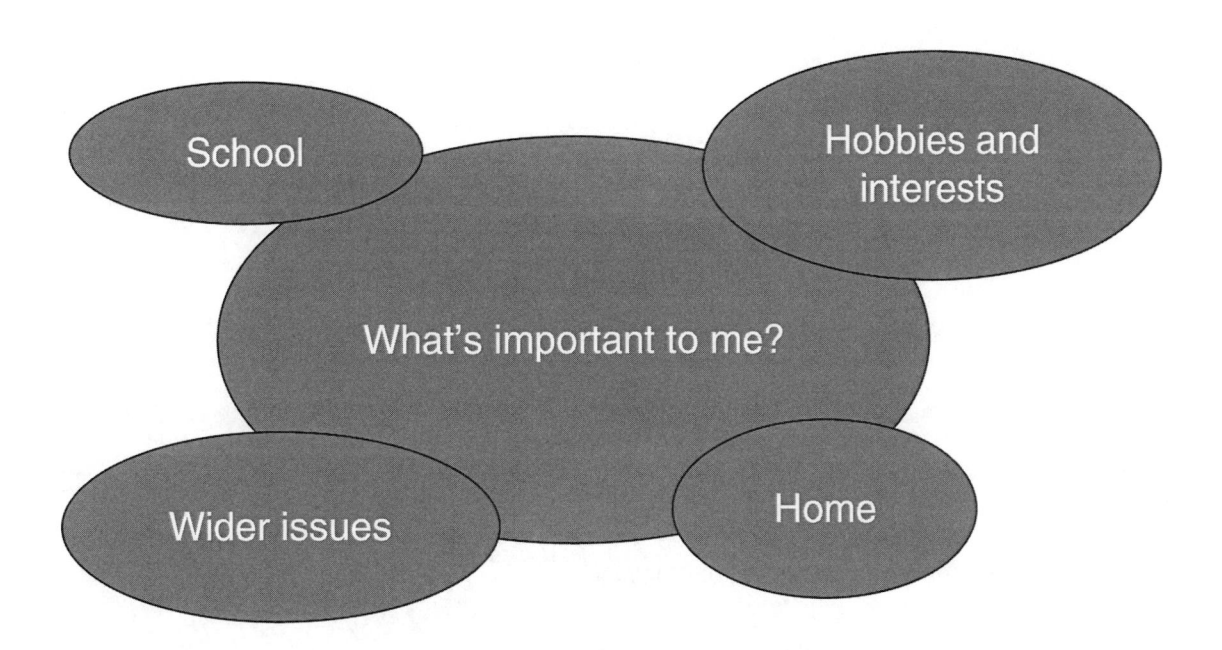

EDUCATING AND SUPPORTING AUTISTIC GIRLS

4. Journal keeping

For: Students

Instructions: You might like to suggest students keep a journal. It can be useful for some as a way to understand and manage their thoughts and emotions. Remind students that a journal is confidential and does not have to be shared with you or anybody else. You might like to give them the following guidance.

Keeping a journal

Keeping a journal can help you to make sense of events and reflect on your feelings. You can also write about things you have done well, things you have learned and what you are looking forward to. Why not give it a try? It might be something you enjoy or find useful.

```
Date:
My thoughts:…
```

Use a special journal, a notebook or a digital device.

Write in it as often or as little as you like.

Use words, pictures, diagrams or whatever you like.

Make it colourful if you like.

Don't worry about spelling, punctuation or grammar.

Write about the things you've enjoyed and done well.

Write about your worries and anxieties.

Write about your thoughts and feelings.

You don't have to share your journal with anybody. It's a private space just for you.

Remember! If you need more support with an issue, ask a trusted adult for help – perhaps a family member, a teacher, mentor or counsellor.

PART 4: PRACTICAL RESOURCES

Autism and Me

For: Students/service users

Instructions: Use this outline to help a student explore what autism means to them. Help the student find reliable sources of information to answer any questions they might have.

Autism and me

Getting a diagnosis of autism can be a confusing time. You might be relieved that there is an explanation for your differences and difficulties. You might feel sad, angry, in denial, annoyed, happy, or many other emotions. That's ok. Use this sheet to record some of your thoughts, feelings and worries.

Your initial thoughts and feelings about receiving a diagnosis of autism:

Do you already know anything about autism? How would you describe it to a friend?

What else would you like to know about autism? Make a list of any questions here. Then ask a trusted adult to help you find the answers from reliable sources.

Some autistic individuals have intense interests or hobbies. Do you have anything you feel passionate about? What do you love most about this?

Copyright material from Victoria Honeybourne (2024), *Educating and Supporting Autistic Girls*, Routledge

Some autistic people are over- or under-sensitive to lights, noise, touch, tastes or smells. Do you have any sensory sensitivities? What do you like and what do you find distressing?

Light:

Noise:

Smells:

Taste:

Touch/textures:

What positive qualities or strengths do you have relating to your autism? (e.g. a good attention to detail, good focus, a sense of justice)

What do you find difficult because of your autism? Consider home, school and hobbies.

What are the positives about being different to others?

Who is in your support network? Who are the people you can talk to about autism? Consider family, friends, teachers, mentors, counsellors or other professionals. Would you like to meet other autistic people? If so, are there any groups in your local area?

PART 4: PRACTICAL RESOURCES

5. My strengths and skills

For: Students

Instructions: Discuss the following strengths with students. Maybe they can think of more to add. Ask students to identify their top strengths. Can they give examples of having used these strengths?

Strengths and skills. Some suggested definitions.

Enthusiastic You do things with energy and enthusiasm. You put effort in.	**Energetic** You have lots of energy, like to get things done and keep busy.	**Grateful** You are thankful for the good things that happen.	**Hopeful** You expect the best in the future and work hard to achieve it.
Kind You look after, help or do nice things for other people.	**Honest** You tell the truth and do not exaggerate.	**Love of learning** You love learning new things and finding out new information.	**Curiosity** You are interested in new things and ask questions.
Creative You are original and find new ways of doing things.	**Forgiving** You forgive yourself and other people when you or they make a mistake.	**Leadership** You can direct and organise activities and encourage others to join in.	**Perseverance** You try hard to overcome difficulties and don't give up easily.
Determination You finish what you start and reach your goals.	**Humour** You can see the funny side when it is appropriate.	**Teamwork** You work well with others, each taking a fair share of the work.	**Independence** You work well by yourself and take responsibility for yourself.
Brave You try to overcome threats and challenges.	**Spiritual** You have beliefs which help to shape the way you live.	**Fair** You give everybody a fair chance, regardless of your personal opinion.	**Self-control** You can control your behaviour and actions when necessary.
Optimistic You are hopeful and see the positive side of things.	**Careful** You consider risks carefully and do not do anything that could be dangerous.	**Socially aware** You are aware of the thoughts and feelings of other people and of social situations.	**Environmentally aware** You care about the impact of your actions on the environment.

Copyright material from Victoria Honeybourne (2024), *Educating and Supporting Autistic Girls*, Routledge

Appreciative You are able to appreciate and value other people's contributions or able to appreciate little things in everyday life.	Loving You value close relationships with your family and friends.	Evaluative You are able to examine a problem from many points of view and weigh up the evidence.	Emotionally aware You are aware of your emotions and where they have come from.
Open-minded You respect other people's opinions and take their views into consideration.	Responsible You can be trusted to do things sensibly and know the difference between right and wrong.	Reliable You can be trusted to do what you say you will.	Modest You do not brag or boast about yourself.
Supportive You support and encourage other people to do well.	Generous You share your time, energy, knowledge or belongings with others.	Attention to detail You notice small details and patterns. You do all parts of a job.	Connection with animals You care about and look after animals.

My strengths, skills and talents. What are your strengths, skills and talents? Fill them in here. You might also find it useful to ask other people what they think your strengths are.

My strengths:	Examples of when I've used these strengths:

PART 4: PRACTICAL RESOURCES

Learning

The next set of resources have been designed to support the learning processes as well as executive functioning skills. These activities are designed to be adapted for use across a range of subjects and settings, rather than being subject specific.

1. Learning self-audit

For: Students

Instructions: Use this self-audit to identify what aspects of learning you are good at, what you would like to develop further and what you need more support with.

	☹	😐	☺
I bring the right equipment and books to school/college.			
I hand my homework in on time.			
I listen to and remember what the teacher is saying.			
I understand the instructions and what I have to do.			
I work well independently.			
I ask for help with my work when I need it.			
I work well with a partner.			
I work well in a small group.			
I contribute answers in class.			
I plan my work before I begin it.			
I present my work so it is easy to understand.			
I use computers effectively to help me present my work.			
I give presentations in front of the class.			
I enjoy writing longer pieces.			
I can use the Internet effectively for research.			
I check my work for mistakes before I hand it in.			
I act on feedback given about my work.			
I concentrate on my work in lessons.			
My learning strengths are:	**Areas I'd like support with:**		

EDUCATING AND SUPPORTING AUTISTIC GIRLS

2. Timetable

For: Students

Instructions: Write in your subjects, the room number and the time of your lessons. Remember to include breaks and lunchtimes too. Colour-code if you feel it is helpful.

Lesson and time	Monday	Tuesday	Wednesday	Thursday	Friday

PART 4: PRACTICAL RESOURCES

3. Things to take to school

For: Students

Instructions: Use this sheet to help you remember what to pack in your bag. Keep it somewhere you see it every evening or morning when you are getting your things ready. Tick off each item when you have put it in your bag. You might like to laminate it and use a wipe-clean pen so that you can re-use it each week.

Every day				

Every week				
Monday	**Tuesday**	**Wednesday**	**Thursday**	**Friday**

This week				
Monday	**Tuesday**	**Wednesday**	**Thursday**	**Friday**

EDUCATING AND SUPPORTING AUTISTIC GIRLS

4. Task planner

For: Students (some students will find it beneficial to work through these with an adult, until they learn how to complete them independently)

Instructions: Breaking down a task can make it seem more manageable and help you to decide what to do first. Decide on the steps you need to take and what you need for each task. Remember to include steps such as proof-reading or checking your work before you hand it in.

My task is			Date due:
Steps I need to take:	Equipment or support needed:	By when or how long:	Done:

PART 4: PRACTICAL RESOURCES

5. Choosing the right idea

For: Students (some students will benefit from working with an adult until they learn how to complete this exercise independently)

Instructions: Writing the pros and cons of each of your ideas can help you decide which one to take further. This might be useful for school projects or making choices outside of school too.

My Task: _____

Idea 1:	Pros
	Cons
Idea 2:	Pros
	Cons
Idea 3:	Pros
	Cons

The idea I have chosen is _____ because _____.

6. Story planner

For: Students

Instructions: Write or draw the main events of your story in the grid below. This is just a planning sheet so don't worry about crossing things out, moving things around or making mistakes. This planning sheet can help you to decide on the events of your story and the best order, before you begin to write it properly.

Setting – include useful words or phrases that describe where the story takes place:	Characters – who are the main characters in your story? Describe them briefly.

Beginning: What will be an interesting beginning?			
			Ending: A satisfactory conclusion that explains what happens to the characters.

7. Essay planners

For: Students (some students will benefit from working through these with adults until they are able to complete them independently)

Instructions: Planning your essays will help you to include all of the main points in the right order. Make notes about what you will include in each section. Don't worry about crossings out, mistakes or full sentences at this point. Use this sheet while writing as a reminder of what you want to include in which order.

(a) 'Argument' style essay

Title or question

Introduction (An introduction explains what the topic of your essay is and gives a brief explanation of what you will discuss.)

Arguments for

Arguments against

Conclusion (The conclusion summarises the main points made in your essay and comes to a conclusion about the initial question.)

(b) Newspaper/magazine article

Headline/Title

Introduction (Who, what, why, when, where)

Paragraph 1

Paragraph 2

Paragraph 3

Conclusion/Outro/Summary

PART 4: PRACTICAL RESOURCES

8. Group work planning

For: Students and staff. Older students might be able to divide up the work by themselves. Younger students will benefit from an adult supporting them to plan and share out the work.

Instructions: This sheet can help your group plan the work for your group task. Break the task down into smaller chunks. Decide who will do each task and what equipment or help that person/people will need. Those with shorter tasks can help others once they have finished.

Our task			Due date
Jobs to be done	**Who**	**Equipment or help needed**	**By when**
How we will check we are on track			

9. Group work rules

(a) Group work guidelines examples

For: Staff to facilitate discussion among students

Instructions: Share this example of some 'rules' for a group discussion or task. Ask students to discuss questions such as: Why do you think each one is important? Are there any guidelines you would like to add? You might also like to use this list with neurodivergent students on an individual/small-group basis for them to identify and discuss any difficulties that they have with group tasks.

Group work

These are some ideas for when taking part in a group task or discussion:

- Show that you are listening when other people are talking by avoiding distractions and staying quiet.
- Take turns to speak.
- Ask politely when you have not understood what another person said.
- Make your contributions relevant to what is being discussed.
- If you want to disagree with what somebody is saying, do so politely.
- Respect other people's opinions.
- Ensure that everybody is able to contribute to the discussion or the work in whatever way that they can.
- Avoid personal insults and offensive language.
- Do a fair share of the work.
- Let others know if you have a problem doing your part of the task.
- Help others in the group if they don't understand, need support or encounter a problem.

(b) Group-discussion roles

For: Classroom resource for teachers/teaching assistants

Instructions: In a group discussion, it can help to allocate each person a specific task, although it is also important that everybody contributes to the discussion. Here are some examples of specific tasks that might be given to individuals within a group. Add other roles if relevant to different tasks. The role cards might support some students to be able to contribute or to stay on task.

Timekeeper The timekeeper keeps the group to time. She will allocate a set amount of time to discuss each task or question and tell the group when it is time to move on. She will also tell the group when it is almost time to finish.	**Note taker** The note taker writes down the main points that have been raised by the group so that the group has a record of what was discussed or agreed.
Chair or coordinator The chair or coordinator leads the group and makes sure that the group stays on task. She ensures that everybody contributes. She brings the group back to the task at hand.	**Summariser** The summariser makes a summary at the end of the task to summarise what has been discussed and check that everybody agrees.
Presenter The presenter presents the group's findings to the rest of the class in a clear way.	**Checker** The checker is responsible for checking the group's work as they go along. She checks that the group is doing the right thing and has completed all parts of a task.
Materials manager The materials manager is responsible for gathering the equipment needed and returning it at the end of the task.	**Encourager** The encourager's role is to encourage all members of the group to contribute. She will encourage others not only to take part but also to bring up any problems and support each other.

10. Presentations

(a) Planning sheet

For: Students

Instructions: Use this planning sheet to help you to plan your presentation. Start by organising your thoughts regarding the content of your presentation. Rehearse what you want to include for each point. Consider the visuals you might use to support what you are saying (such as a poster or slide show).

Topic
Introduction (What are you going to say to introduce the topic? You need to tell your audience what you will talk about and the points you are going to cover.)
Main points (Make notes of the points you will cover.) 1. 2. 3. 4.
Conclusion (How will you summarise what you have said and come to a conclusion?)
Visuals If you are using a PowerPoint, check that: • Your slides are structured in the right order. • Your writing is big enough for the audience to see. • Your writing is clear and can be seen on the background. • You just put the main points on the slides and don't just read the slides aloud. You should talk about each point in more detail. • Pictures or video links are clear and relevant.
Props • Do you need any other props or objects to show to the audience?
Cue cards • Are you going to make small cue cards or notes to refer to when you are speaking?

(b) Presentations checklist

Practising your presentation is an important part of feeling prepared. Ask a friend, family member or mentor to watch you practise and fill in this sheet to help you see what you need to work on. Alternatively, you could video yourself and watch it back, filling in the sheet yourself about your own performance.

Did I		Comments
speak loudly enough?		
speak slowly and clearly so that everybody could understand?		
vary my voice and intonation to make my speech interesting?		
look at the audience and not just my notes?		
use gesture and facial expression appropriately to add to my points?		
explain any complex words or new ideas that the audience might not know?		
keep to the topic?		
give enough detail so that the audience understood, but not too much to bore them?		
have a clear introduction?		
make my points in a sensible order?		
have a clear ending?		
refer to any pictures or props?		
have a clear slide show or other visuals that could be understood?		

11. Revision planner

For: Students

Instructions: We often have to revise for tests, exams or assessments. Revision means revisiting the work we have covered in lessons so that it is fresher in our minds for the exam. We learn best by revising actively rather than passively. Some revision ideas are below. Can you add any ideas of your own?

Doing past exam questions and comparing your answers to the marking scheme	Making a mind map or spider diagram of the topic
Testing yourself on a topic	Asking another person to test you on a topic
Explaining a topic to somebody else and answering questions on it	Teaching somebody else a topic
Doing online revision tests and activities	Watching a video clip about the topic
Making a presentation about the topic to other people	Making a poster about a topic
Reading over your notes, annotating and highlighting key points	Reorganising and summarising notes from lessons
Making and playing a game or quiz about the topic	Practising doing timed essays or questions in preparation for the exam
Discussing a topic with other people, revising the same thing and questioning each other	Using revision guides and study guides

Revision. Use this planning sheet to plan the revision you need to do for your upcoming exams.

Topic to revise	Revision strategies to use	By when	Done?

PART 4: PRACTICAL RESOURCES

Transitions and moving on

The following resources are designed to aid the transition process for autistic students.

1. Transition to new settings

For: Students transferring to a new setting, e.g. from primary to secondary school, from secondary school to college, or from one school to another. Students will get most benefit if they work through this with an adult who then supports them to find out the answers to their questions and worries.

Instructions: Use the following sheet to organise your thoughts and feelings about transition.

Name:	Name of new setting:
What I am looking forward to in my new setting:	What I am worried about in my new setting:
Questions I want to ask about the new setting: 1. 2. 3. 4. 5. 6. 7. 8.	Answers I have found out (using a website, visiting new setting, asking others who attend, speaking to members of staff, attending open evenings, etc.)
Things I need to do before I start my new setting (e.g. attend an Open Day, attend a taster day, meet the SENCO):	

Copyright material from Victoria Honeybourne (2024), *Educating and Supporting Autistic Girls*, Routledge

EDUCATING AND SUPPORTING AUTISTIC GIRLS

2. Investigating future courses of study

For: Students

Instructions: Use this template to consider what to ask on open days or college visits.

Visiting a college or university

Use this sheet to make a note of things you would like to find out or ask before visiting a college or university.

You might want to consider

- the different courses or levels available
- how the course is assessed
- how the course is taught or which learning activities you will be expected to take part in
- if there is a practical element or work placement
- support available to help you with your studies
- extracurricular activities and clubs on offer
- accommodation available if you are living away from home
- support with independent living or social skills.

Questions I need to ask/things to find out:	Answers I've found:

Copyright material from Victoria Honeybourne (2024), *Educating and Supporting Autistic Girls*, Routledge

3. Independent living

For: Students

Instructions: If you are moving away from home for the first time, there are many things that you will have to do for yourself. Take a look at this list. How confident do you feel about each one? If there are any you are not sure about, how will you improve at these? Are there any other things you would like to add to the list?

Task	☹	😐	☺	Steps I can take to learn this
Washing my clothes				
Cooking my meals				
Going grocery shopping				
Washing up				
Keeping my rooms clean				
Personal hygiene				
Getting up on time				
Using money				
Keeping to a budget				
Using my bank account				
Getting to places on time				
Eating healthily, doing exercise and getting enough sleep				
Keeping my belongings safe				
Keeping myself safe				

4. Careers coaching for autism

For: Autistic individuals considering careers options

Instructions: Read the following information and consider the questions.

Considering careers

Deciding what you want to do can be a tricky decision. You might not be able to decide between a few things you are interested in, or you might know roughly what we are interested in (education, health, ICT) but not know which role you are best suited for. Or you might have no idea at all at this point.

Everybody will have a different ideal job. What will suit one person, won't suit another, as everybody has different skills, strengths and values. It's important to consider what will suit you as an individual. It's also important to remember that you don't have to make a decision for life. Many people change job roles or careers many times throughout their lives and some have a 'portfolio career' of two or more roles that they do part-time. Many people try a few things before they find what suits them best. You can never predict what opportunities might come up in the future, what new interests you might develop, or how the world of work will change.

There are many options:

(a) Looking for a job and becoming employed by another person or company.

(b) Self-employment is when you work for yourself or have your own business (e.g. your own gardening business or your own mobile hairdressing business).

(c) Being a freelancer is when you take on different projects for different people at different times (e.g. many people in the creative industries work on a freelance basis).

(d) An apprenticeship is where you learn on the job and usually have some time in the week to gain a related qualification.

(e) Some people choose to work part-time and study part-time, so they can do both things at once.

PART 4: PRACTICAL RESOURCES

(a) Consider the type of job that suits you

First consider what sort of job you are looking for and what would suit you. Being clear on what you want can help you to make the right decision for you. Make notes on the following points:

Do you want to work mainly indoors or outdoors?	
What sort of environment do you want to work in? Consider your sensory needs: busy, quiet, crowded, brightly lit, naturally lit, etc.	
Do you want to work mainly independently or in a team?	
Do you want a job where there is lots of interaction with other people (customers and clients)?	
Do you want a desk-based job, or do you want something more active?	
Do you want to work the same days each week, or are you happy working on a rota?	
Do you want to work office hours (roughly 9 am–5 pm) or are you happy to work shifts, including evenings and weekends?	
Do you want to work close to where you live or are you happy to commute further away?	
Are you limited by transport options?	
Do you want a set workplace, or would you like to work in different places each day?	
Do you want a job that is the same every day, or do you want a job in which every day is different?	
Do you want a job that is done in work hours, or a job that you have work to do in your own time?	
Do you want to wear your own clothes or a uniform?	
Do you want to gain more qualifications while you're working?	
Do you want opportunities for promotion and to gain different responsibilities?	

EDUCATING AND SUPPORTING AUTISTIC GIRLS

(b) Consider your strengths and skills

People are often happiest when they are doing something that makes use of their strengths and skills and that is in line with their personal values.

Start by considering the following questions:

What are you interested in? (e.g. hobbies, interests, school subjects, topics)	What qualifications do you have? (include those gained outside of school too)
What skills do you have? (e.g. technology skills, public speaking, sports coaching, looking after animals)	What are your strengths? (e.g. work well independently, well-organised)
When do you feel happiest? (e.g. which activities and environments)	What drains your energy? (e.g. too much socialising, sensory input)

(c) Consider your values

Being clearer about your personal values can help you to make decisions that are meaningful and right for you. Consider the following list of values. Add your own to the list if there are other words that better describe your values. Circle those that resonate with you. Choose your top five values – the things that are most important to you at this point. Some values might stay constant throughout our lives, while others may change with growth and life experiences. Knowing your top values might help you consider careers that are meaningful to you.

Accomplishment	Achievement	Adventure	Ambition
Art	Awe	Belonging	Calmness
Carefulness	Challenge	Cheerfulness	Community
Creativity	Curiosity	Determination	Encouragement
Energy	Enjoyment	Environment	Expertise
Fairness	Family	Freedom	Friendship
Fun	Generosity	Humour	Independence
Individuality	Integrity	Kindness	Knowledge
Making a difference	Nature	Open-mindedness	Religion
Spirituality	Volunteering	Commitment	Connection
Emotional health	Honesty	Joy	Loyalty
Personal growth	Solitude	Power	Recognition
Risk-taking	Self-expression	Security	Trust
Tolerance	Learning	Resilience	Justice

5. First day on the job

For: Autistic individuals about to start work experience, voluntary work or employment

Instructions: There are lots of things to learn and find out when you begin a new job. Don't be afraid to ask questions and to ask for help if you need it. Consider what you might need to know on your first day in a new role. Look at this list and add anything else you can think of that might be relevant. Take this checklist with you so that you remember to ask what you want to find out.

What time do you start and finish work?	
Do you have to sign in or sign out anywhere?	
What time do you have breaks or lunch?	
Where can you spend breaks and lunch?	
Where are the toilets and staff lockers?	
Who should you speak to if you need help or have a question?	
Do you need a uniform or what type of clothing should you wear?	
Are there any health and safety procedures you need to be aware of?	
What is the procedure if there is a fire drill?	
What are your colleagues' names and roles?	
(If you drive) Where is it best to park?	
What should you do if you are ill and unable to come to work?	
Do you need to learn how to use any equipment (e.g. photocopier, till, computers)?	
What is the procedure for tea and coffee (e.g. does everybody bring their own, is there a kitty, do you take turns)?	

PART 4: PRACTICAL RESOURCES

6. Disclosure

For: Autistic individuals considering work placements, voluntary work or employment

Instructions: A planning sheet for autistic individuals to consider how and when they want to disclose their autism. Some students might benefit from working through this sheet with a mentor or careers advisor for extra guidance.

Disclosing your autism

Whether you tell anyone about your autism (also called 'disclosing' your autism) is a matter of personal preference. Under current UK legislation, you can tell an employer about a disability at any point, before, during or after the recruitment process. So, it is up to you when you decide to tell your employer about your autism. If you do tell your employer, it is their responsibility to keep it confidential and not tell your colleagues, unless you want them to.

Possible reasons to disclose:

- You might not be entitled to workplace support until you have disclosed your autism. Without having some knowledge of autism, employers and colleagues might struggle to help you meet your needs. Employers and colleagues might be more supportive and understanding if there are certain tasks you find more challenging or need extra support with.
- You might need 'reasonable adjustments' in the workplace under the Equality Act (2010). You can only request these once you have disclosed your autism.
- Colleagues might be more understanding that you work, socialise and interpret the world in different ways.
- You might feel more comfortable knowing that your employer and colleagues are aware of your autism. It might mean you feel more able to be yourself and feel less concerned about having to hide sensory sensitivities, stimming or other aspects of your autism.
- You might feel that being autistic gives you an advantage in your job role.
- You value being different and feel it is important for neurodivergent individuals to be more visible in the workplace and in other aspects of life.

Some people worry about disclosing their autism. Some concerns can include:

- Worry that employers might not want to employ or promote autistic individuals because of prejudices and stereotypes.
- Worry that colleagues might think you are treated differently.
- Worry that colleagues might assume you have certain traits or difficulties or will treat you differently if they know about your autism. Or you might worry about not being believed as others might not immediately see your difficulties.

Copyright material from Victoria Honeybourne (2024), *Educating and Supporting Autistic Girls*, Routledge

You might choose not to disclose that you have autism and that is your choice. It might not be important to you, or you might feel that it doesn't affect you in your current role. However, it's important to remember that the Equality Act (2010) does make it unlawful to discriminate against somebody because of a disability. If you feel you are discriminated against because of being autistic you should bring this up with the relevant person (often a manager or HR).

Planning to disclose:

Consider the following questions to help you decide when and how to disclose.

1. *What are your initial thoughts or worries about disclosing your autism?*

...

...

...

2. *Possible or current difficulties or challenges in this role:*

You might find it useful to consider the difficulties you face (or think you might face) in your job role. For each one consider what you could do to improve this (e.g. work in a quieter part of the office, have time to read information before meetings, ask for autism training for your colleagues). Thinking about these things in advance might mean a meeting with your employer is more productive and focused on solutions.

Difficulties/Challenges	**Possible solutions?**

PART 4: PRACTICAL RESOURCES

3. *When are you going to disclose?*

Decide on when is the most appropriate time (on an application form, before an interview, during an interview, after being offered a job). This is very much personal preference and depends on how your autism affects you. You might, for example, need reasonable adjustments in place to attend an interview, in which case, it makes sense to disclose before this.

…

…

…

4. *How are you going to disclose?*

Are you going to ask for a face-to-face meeting, write it in an e-mail, or bring it up at the start/end of your interview? Are you comfortable speaking to your employer alone or do you prefer to ask a support worker to accompany you?

…

…

…

5. *What are you going to say?*

You might want to start by explaining your diagnosis and why you are telling them. You might want to consider aspects of the role that you will find difficult or the reasonable adjustments that you will need. You might not know at this point what adjustments you will need and that is fine – if you have told your employer about your autism, it might be easier to bring this up in future once you know. You might also explain the strategies that you use to overcome difficulties and how these help you (e.g. making notes of oral explanations, wearing ear plugs in noisy environments). Remember also to mention the positives! You are an individual with many strengths and skills so don't forget to mention these too!

…

…

…

Copyright material from Victoria Honeybourne (2024), *Educating and Supporting Autistic Girls*, Routledge

EDUCATING AND SUPPORTING AUTISTIC GIRLS

6. *Getting further support*

Some employers will have more awareness and understanding of autism than others. You might want to research where you or your employer can get more support so that you can signpost your employer to this (e.g. the Access to Work scheme, factsheets from local autism organisations).

...

....

...

PART 4: PRACTICAL RESOURCES

Anxiety and wellbeing

The final set of resources consider wellbeing and the impact of anxiety. Individuals experiencing anxiety or other mental health needs should be referred to the relevant professional as soon as possible and these activities are not intended as a substitute for therapy and might not be suitable for all. They are intended as a way for some individuals to explore their thoughts, feelings and wellbeing and to take positive steps to improve their wellbeing.

1. What went well?

For: Students

Instructions: Some students might have a tendency to dwell on the negatives. Encouraging them to notice the positives might help them to develop a more balanced view.

What's going well?

Keep a record of the positives! It might be things that you have done well ('I decorated an amazing cake for my brother's birthday'), things you have improved at ('I did my homework to get it out the way'), things you enjoyed ('I loved Lego club at lunchtime') or things you are grateful for ('My friend saved me a seat at lunchtime'). Try to find three each day.

Day	What went well?
Monday	
Tuesday	
Wednesday	
Thursday	
Friday	
Saturday	
Sunday	

PART 4: PRACTICAL RESOURCES

2. What makes me happy?

For: Students

Instructions: Consider all of the things that bring you happiness, joy, or a feeling of calm and wellbeing. This might include some of your hobbies, interests and favourite activities. It might include pleasurable sensory experiences, like touching a favourite soft blanket or listening to calming music. It might include being with a favourite person or pet or being by yourself. Use this as a reminder of the things you can do on a daily basis to help you feel better.

Things that bring me joy, happiness or calm.

3. Reflecting on events, experiences and misunderstandings

For: Students to work through with a mentor or key worker

Instructions: Autistic students might have difficulty interpreting something that has happened. Creating a storyboard of the event might be beneficial for some students. First, ask them to draw out the events in the form of a storyboard or cartoon strip (stick people are fine!). Then use these drawings to discuss what happened. Use speech bubbles and thought bubbles to find out what the individual was saying/thinking/feeling and to explore what others might have been thinking/feeling. This might help you be able to understand the situation from the student's perspective and for the student to understand the situation from the other person's perspective.

You might want to use some of these in your storyboard:

In the *speech bubbles*, you can write what different people are saying.

In the *thought bubbles*, you can write what people are thinking.

PART 4: PRACTICAL RESOURCES

Explosions and other shapes can be used for words such as 'Bang!', 'Surprise!' or 'Wow!'

What happened?		

Explosions and other shapes can be used for words such as 'Bang!', 'Surprise!' or 'Wow!'

4. Emotions diary

For: Students. Some might benefit from discussing their findings with a trusted adult afterwards.

Instructions: There are no right or wrong feelings; we all experience a range of feelings every day. Feelings come and go all the time. Sometimes we might identify a trigger for a certain feeling (e.g. feeling anxious just before an exam) but other times we might not be able to identify an obvious trigger. This template might help you begin to notice and label some of your feelings. It doesn't matter if you don't have a word to describe how you are feeling; often we find it difficult to define our feelings or feel a mix of things all at once.

Feelings words you might like to choose from (or use your own):

Happy, sad, angry, furious, calm, frustrated, annoyed, irritated, upset, excited, anxious, worried, surprised, shocked, scared, optimistic, pessimistic, overwhelmed, bored, fed up, hurt, shy, embarrassed, confident, grateful, interested, delighted, sympathetic, empathetic, lonely, energetic, playful, impulsive, spontaneous, helpful, kind, peaceful, comfortable, pleased, loving, disappointed, discouraged, guilty, uncertain, empty, indecisive, suspicious, nervous.

Date	Feelings noticed	Notes (What was the situation? Did you notice anything happening in your body?)

PART 4: PRACTICAL RESOURCES

5. Challenging unhelpful thoughts

For: Students to work through with a trusted adult

Instructions: Sometimes we experience unhelpful thoughts. For example, a friend might walk past you in a shop without saying anything. Immediately you might have a thought of: 'My friend deliberately ignored me. She obviously doesn't want to be my friend any more. I must have done something to upset her'. Your mind has jumped to conclusions. In reality, it might have been that your friend didn't see you, or was worrying about something so not taking in her surroundings, or had headphones in and so didn't hear you call her name. Some people find it useful to notice their thoughts and then to consider what a more helpful, rational thought could be instead (e.g. 'I know I've not done anything to upset my friend. She just didn't notice me today.').

Situation	Automatic thought	A more helpful thought could be:

Copyright material from Victoria Honeybourne (2024), *Educating and Supporting Autistic Girls*, Routledge

6. Reaching my goals

For: Students/service users

Instructions: You might have a goal you would like to reach (like revising regularly until your exams, or attending a dance class, or learning how to do something independently). Some people can find it helpful to break their goal down into smaller steps and to consider possible barriers to them achieving their goal. This can help them to plan more effectively. You might like to use the following template.

My goal is:	
(Try to make your goal as specific and as realistic as possible)	
The smaller steps I need to take to reach my goal are: 1. 2. 3. 4. 5. 6.	
What are my strengths and skills that could be useful in this situation?	Have I been successful doing something similar in the past? What helped this success?
What barriers or obstacles might get in my way?	How could I overcome these obstacles?
Who could I ask for help in this situation?	Why is this goal important to me?

References

ADHD UK (2023) *ADHD Incidence.* Available from: adhduk.co.uk/adhd-incidence/ [accessed on 14 February 2023].

BDA (2023a) *About dyslexia.* Available from: www.bdadyslexia.org.uk/dyslexia [accessed 14 February 2023].

BDA (2023b) *About dyscalculia.* Available from: www.bdadyslexia.org.uk/dyscalculia/how-can-i-identify-dyscalculia [accessed 14 February 2023].

Dyspraxia Foundation (2023) *Dyspraxia at a Glance.* Available from: dyspraxiafoundation.org.uk/what_is_dyspraxia/dyspraxia-at-a-glance/ [accessed on 14 February 2023].

National Autistic Society (2023) *What is autism?* Available from: www.autism.org.uk/advice-and-guidance/what-is-autism [accessed on 14 February 2023].

Simone R. (2010) *Aspergirls.* London: Jessica Kingsley Publishers.

Spectrum Gaming (2022) *Do you understand your anxiety?* Available from: barrierstoeducation.co.uk/understanding-anxiety [accessed 14 February 2023].

Further reading and resources

There are an increasing number of books being written for children and young adults with neurodivergent protagonists, with a growing proportion written by neurodivergent authors (#OwnVoices). This list is just a small selection, but check in a local library or bookshop for the latest releases.

Middle grade and young adult fiction books containing autistic characters

Frankie's World by Aoife Dooley (autistic author)

A Kind of Spark and *Show Us Who You Are* by Elle McNicholl (autistic author)

PAWS by Kate Foster (autistic author)

Can you see me?, *Ways to be me* and *Do you know me?* All by Libby Scott and Rebecca Westcott

The State of Grace by Rachael Lucas (autistic author)

M is for Autism by Vicky Martin and the students of Limpsfield Grange School

Me and Sam-Sam Handle the Apocalypse by Susan Vaught

The Many Mysteries of the Finkel Family by Sarah Kapit

For younger children

Talking is not my thing by Rose Robbins

I am an Aspie Girl by Danuta Bulhak-Paterson

Ellie Needs to Go: A book about how to use public toilets safely for girls and young women with autism and related conditions by Kate E. Reynolds

Non-fiction books about autism and neurodiversity for young people

A Different Sort of Normal by Abigail Balfe (2021, Puffin Books, London) – an autobiographical account of growing up undiagnosed on the autism spectrum which includes lots of information about autism and gender identity.

The Spectrum Girl's Survival Guide: How to grow up awesome and autistic by Siena Castellon

(2020, Jessica Kingsley Publisher's, London)

Wired Differently: 30 Neurodivergent People You Should Know, by Joe Wells (2022, Jessica Kingsley Publishers, London)

The Reason I Jump by Naoki Higashida

The Autism Friendly Guide to Periods by Robyn Steward

The Independent Woman's Handbook for Super Safe Living on the Autism Spectrum by Robyn Steward

The Girl with the Curly Hair: Asperger's and Me by Alis Rowe

What's happening to Ellie? A book about puberty for girls and young women with autism and related conditions by Kate E. Reynolds

What is sex? A guide for people with autism, special educational needs and disabilities by Kate E. Reynolds

The Autism and Neurodiversity Self-Advocacy Handbook by Barb Cook and Yenn Purkis

Autobiographical accounts by autistic women (for adults)

Odd Girl Out: An autistic woman in a neurotypical world by Laura James (2017, Bluebird, London)

How to be Autistic by Charlotte Amelia Poe (2019, Myriad Editions, Oxford)

Drama Queen by Sara Gibbs (2022, Hachette, London)

Ten Steps to Nanatte by Hannah Gadsby

On autism in females

Spectrum Women Walking to the Beat of Autism by Barb Cook and Michelle Garnett

Camouflage: The Hidden Lives of Autistic Women by Dr Sarah Bargiela, 2019, Jessica Kingsley Publishers, London

Girls and Autism: Educational, Family and Personal Perspectives edited by Barry Carpenter, Francesca Happe and Jo Egerton

Gender Identity, Sexuality and Autism: Voices from across the Spectrum, by Eva Mendes and Meredith Maroney

Safeguarding Autistic Girls: Strategies for Professionals, by Carly Jones

The Guide to Good Mental Health on the Autism Spectrum by Jeanette Purkis, Dr Emma Goodall and Dr Jane Nugent

Supporting Spectacular Girls: A Practical Guide to supporting autistic girls wellbeing and self-esteem by Helen Clarke

On PDA

Being Julia: A personal account of living with PDA by Ruth Fidler and Julia Daunt

The PDA Paradox by Harry Thompson

I'm not upside down, I'm downside up by Harry Thompson

Me and my PDA: A guide to PDA for young people by Tamar Levi and Gloria Dura-Vila

PDA by PDAers: From anxiety to avoidance and masking to meltdowns, edited by Sally Cat

The Teacher's Introduction to Pathological Demand Avoidance: Essential Strategies for the Classroom by Clare Truman

Collaborative Approaches to Learning for Pupils with PDA by Ruth Fidler and Phil Christie

Understanding Pathological Demand Avoidance Syndrome in Children: A guide for parents, teachers and other professionals by Phil Christie, Margaret Duncan, Zara Healy and Ruth Fidler

Useful Organisations

National Autistic Society

Leading UK autism charity. Informative website with information, resources and training: autism.org.uk

Pathological Demand Avoidance (PDA)

PDA Society, www.pdasociety.org.uk

UK charity with informative website of information, resources and case studies about PDA.

Selective mutism

SMIRA – Selective Mutism Information and Research Association, selectivemutism.org.uk

Mental health

Young Minds www.youngminds.org.uk

UK charity with an informative website for children and young people about mental health, as well as for parents and professionals.

Young Stonewall www.youngstonewall.org.uk

A charity campaigning for equality and fair treatment for LGBTQIA+ people and against discrimination.

FURTHER READING AND RESOURCES

Neurodiversity

British Dyslexia Association

www.bdadyslexia.org.uk

Dyspraxia Foundation

www.dyspraxiafoundation.org.uk

ADHD Foundation

www.adhdfoundation.org.uk

ADHD UK

Adhduk.co.uk

IPSEA – Independent Provider of Special Education Advice

Ipsea.org.uk

Autism Education Trust

Autismeducationtrust.org.uk

Index

absence from school 72–3, 75–6
ADHD 22, 40, 86, 115
ADHD UK 115
alexithymia 68
anxiety 18, 21, 23, 43–4, 72–4, 157
Asperger, Hans 13–14
Asperger Syndrome 6, 13–14, 120
Atkinson, M. 76
attitude 86
Attwood, T. xii, 22–3, 58
auditory processing 38
autism: adult 20–1; awareness 20–1, 78, 80, 82; causes 8, 21; definition 16–8; prevalence 20; traits 16–8
Autistica 68

BAE Systems 19
Balfe, Abigail 65, 69, 70, 71, 86, 87
Bargiela, S. 23
BDA (British Dyslexia Association) 115
Begley, J. 53
Book Trust 71
Bristol Autism Support 40
bullying 53, 54, 60, 70–1

careers coaching 148–52
Castano, E. 71
CDC (Centre for Disease Control and Prevention) 20
CIPD (Chartered Institute for Personnel and Development) 19
co-production 82, 104
Costley, D. 72
Cuijpers, P. 71
Czech, H. 14

Den Boer, P.C. 71
diagnosis 6, 18, 20, 23–4, 80–1
double empathy problem 47
Dring-Turner, H. 89
DSM-5-TR 14
DXC Technology 19
Dyspraxia Foundation 115

echolalia 52
emotions 68–70, 72–3, 126, 162
empathy 47, 70
executive functioning 40–2

Finkenauer, C. 53
Ford 19
Fortunato, A. 87
friendships 23, 53, 58–60
functioning labels 6, 13, 120

Gadsby, Hannah 55, 64, 74, 78
GCHQ 19
gender: differences 21–3, 86; dysphoria 87; identity 23, 87–8
George, R. 87
Gibbs, Sara 46, 47, 60, 76, 80
Google 19
group work 49–51, 139–40

high-functioning autism (HFA) 6
Hodkinson, A. 15
Hornby, G. 76

identity-first language 6, 120
Idring, S. 4
intense interests *see* special interests
interoception 61

James, Laura 48, 56, 60, 79, 90
Jamison, T.R. 76
Johnstone, D. 15
Joyce, C. 73

Kanner, Leo 13
Kenny, L. 6
Kidd, D. 71
Kranjc, J. 53

Lawrence, C. 45, 57, 90
Lugnegard, T. 72

masking 24, 76–80

INDEX

McGhee, K. 59
McGirl, P. 76
McNicholl, Elle 58
meltdowns 18, 61, 63–4, 84
mental health 15, 21, 23, 78
Microsoft 19
models of disability 15–16
MQ Mental Health Research 21

NAS (National Autistic Society) 16, 20, 87, 115
neurodivergent 6, 7, 16
neurodiversity 7, 15–16; communicating for 109–12
neurodiversity paradigm 7
neurotypical 7, 16

Obaydi, H. 86
Oxford Vaccine Group 21

paralanguage 44–5
pathological demand avoidance (PDA) 14
PDA Society 14
Pellicano, L. 8
person-centred approaches 8
person-first language 6, 120
Poe, Charlotte Amelia 69, 70
positive psychology 8
proprioception 33, 61

repetitive behaviours 17, 23, 73
Rodgers, J. 73

SAP 19
Schuttler, J.O. 76
selective mutism 74–5
self-awareness 9, 122
self-esteem 76

Seligman, M. 8
sensory differences 17, 60–5, 73, 86
sex and relationships education (SRE) 85–9
sexuality 87–8
Shane-Simpson, C. 53
shutdowns 63–4, 84
Simone, R. 24, 59, 66, 86, 122
Skidmore, D. 15
SMIRA 75
social communication 14, 17, 43–9
social interaction *see* social communication
social media 53–6
social mimicry 22
social times 55–8
special interests 22, 66–8
Spectrum Gaming 122
speech, language and communication needs 43
stimming 73
Stokes, M.A. 87
strengths 33–6, 129–30, 150

terminology 6, 120
theory of mind 47–8, 71
Thunberg, Greta 18, 45
transitions 82–5
triad of impairments 13

Urquart, C. 71

values 151
Van Steensel, F.J. 72
Vermeulen, P. 8
visual timetable 40, 42

Wigham, S. 61
Wing, Lorna 13, 21
Winter, M. 45, 57, 90